W9-ABY-239

WITHDRAW

Bramley Library
Salem College
Winston-Salem, NC 27108

WITHDRAWN

Literary Criticism in Perspective: Heinrich Böll

Editorial Board

Literary Criticism in Perspective

James Hardin (South Carolina), General Editor

Eitel Timm (Waldorf School, Vancouver), German Literature

Benjamin Franklin V (South Carolina), American and
English Literature

Reingard M. Nischik (Freiburg im Breisgau), Comparative Literature

About Literary Criticism in Perspective

Books in the series *Literary Criticism in Perspective*, a subseries of *Studies in German Literature, Linguistics, and Culture, and Studies in English and American Literature, Linguistics, and Culture*, trace literary scholarship and criticism on major and neglected writers alike, or on a single major work, a group of writers, a literary school or movement. In so doing the authors — authorities on the topic in question who are also well-versed in the principles and history of literary criticism — address a readership consisting of scholars, students of literature at the graduate and undergraduate level, and the general reader. One of the primary purposes of the series is to illuminate the nature of literary criticism itself, to gauge the influence of social and historic currents on aesthetic judgments once thought objective and normative.

Heinrich Böll: Forty Years of Criticism

Reinhard K. Zachau

Heinrich Böll:
Forty Years of Criticism

CAMDEN HOUSE

Gramley Library
Salem College
Winston-Salem, NC 27108

Copyright © 1994 by
CAMDEN HOUSE, INC.

Published by Camden House, Inc.
Drawer 2025
Columbia, SC 29202 USA

Printed on acid-free paper.
Binding materials are chosen for strength and
durability.

All Rights Reserved
Printed in the United States of America
First Edition

ISBN:1-879751-95-X

LIBRARY OF CONGRESS CATALOGING-IN-PUBLICATION DATA

Zachau, Reinhard K. (Reinhard Konrad))
    Heinrich Böll : forty years of criticism / Reinhard K. Zachau.
        p.   cm.   -- (Literary criticism in perspective)
    Includes bibliographical references and index.
    ISBN 1-879751-95-X (alk. paper)
        1. Böll, Heinrich, 1917-85   --Criticism and interpretation.
I. Title. II. Series.
PT2603.0394Z96 1994
833'.914--dc20

                                                    93-46133
                                                        CIP

Contents

INTRODUCTION

HEINRICH BÖLL WAS A PUBLIC FIGURE in the Germany of the 1970s whose fame eclipsed that of all other writers including Günter Grass. The fascination he exerted both in Germany and abroad originated not only from his books, but also from his captivating personality. Many Germans believed that if they understood the essence of the man and what he stood for, they would be able to comprehend the political atmosphere of the Federal Republic better, especially in the days of turmoil between 1969 and 1975, which to a large degree defined the Federal Republic as we know it now: defiant, where everybody follows political events with intense interest, and at the same time subdued as a result of its dreadful, recent political past. Böll helped shape that image to a large degree, both with his books and with his public appearances.

When in the summer of 1972 Böll received the news that he had been awarded the Nobel Prize for Literature, he responded with the surprised question: "What – me, and not Günter Grass?" ("Was, ich, und nicht Günter Grass?"). This response summarizes Böll's humble self-assessment as a second player to Günter Grass in German post-war literature, a comparison which did not reflect the real picture, although Grass was often regarded as the more literary of the two. Böll's sales figures, however, speak clearly of his success. With thirty-one million books in print translated into forty-five languages, he is by far the most popular of all modern German writers. His unpretentious form and style helped him to become a chronologist of the first forty years of the Federal Republic of Germany. The reader recognizes himself and other people he knows in the characters of Böll's novels. The reader understands the simple ideas of this modest man whose books greatly influenced Germans in understanding their second republic. Böll helped Germans develop a new sense of collective self-hood after their experience with the Nazis. Böll, much against his will, had become so important a public figure in Germany that when a poll of the ten most influential people in West Germany was conducted in the 1970s, Böll was in fourth place, after the politicians Helmut Schmidt, Willy Brandt, and Franz-Josef Strauß, as the man who "represents our conscience" (Amery 1977, 113).

Because he openly attacked social problems, both in his books and in public statements, Heinrich Böll was a controversial writer, admired by his followers and persecuted with the utmost hatred by his conservative antagonists, as in the following statement by Günter Zehm of the conservative daily *Die Welt:*

> Lounging in front of the camera in a sweaty *petite bourgeois* look, one blabbers some "statements". . . all in a very thick dialect, which seems like a parody of proper German, and suggests to the listener he might be watching a Mardi Gras [Carnival] party. . . . (Zehm, in Göttert 1980, 172)[1]

This negative reaction Böll elicited from his conservative countrymen should always be kept in mind. It is especially important when looking at Böll from an American perspective, in which the German-European concept of a political writer does not exist. In order to simplify matters for the American reader, at times the Anglo-American expression *conservative* is used in the present survey to include the political Right in Germany, the Christian Democratic Union and other right-wing parties and schools of thought, and the term *liberal* is applied in a wider sense as meaning anybody connected with parties or ideas of the political Left.

Considering Böll's popularity, this is not the first study on reaction to Böll. The most useful introduction into the Böll reception before 1976 is still Rainer Nägele's book (Nägele 1976), which, along with his article in *New German Critique*, gives a good summary of the first twenty-five years of critical response to Böll. Nägele's introduction was written at the height of the West German discussion on methods which began to focus on reception problems, both historical and aesthetic, and was fueled by Hans Robert Jauß's and Wolfgang Iser's theories, which established the quality of a literary text not as an

---

[1] "Vor die Kamera gefläzt im verschwitzten Kleinbürgerlook, blubbert man irgendwelche 'Statements'. . . das alles im knüppeldicken Dialekt, der im Kontext wie ein Hohn auf die deutsche Hochsprache wirkt und Hörer immer wieder auf den Gedanken bringt, es handle sich um eine karnevalistische Veranstaltung. . . ."

abstract item per se but rather as a quality that takes shape in a reception area established by society (Nägele 1976, 9). Nägele gives first a summary of the history of Böll's work and, more important for our purposes, of critical reaction to his books. The most useful part of Nägele's study is the second part ("Systematischer Teil"), in which each book by Böll is analyzed in detail and various approaches to interpretation are compared. One disadvantage of this approach by Nägele lies in the fact that by his concentrating on the individual novels, critical arguments are taken out of context, and it is almost impossible to appreciate each individual critic. Some of the more important aspects of Nägele's discussion are included and updated in the present survey (such as the "symbol" discussion in *Billiards*). The book concludes with a useful bibliography, as do some other introductions, those by Arnold (1982), Lengning (1962, 1977), and Rademacher (1985). The only shortcoming of Nägele's useful study lies in the fact that it was published in the mid-1970s, before most secondary literature on Böll had appeared.

A bibliography of the most useful books and articles on Böll that are discussed is included in this volume, which is by no means exhaustive, since more than one thousand articles have already been published. However, all independent books about Böll have been included.

A second study concerned with Böll's reception in West Germany came from a team of sociologists that goes by the name *Arbeitsgruppe*. The authors recognized that Böll was more than "just an artist" and that the larger part of his life did not take place in the "artistic dimension," but in the public sphere. By 1975 Böll had become a public institution and was the legitimate subject of public discussion. The researchers from a literature seminar at the University of Tübingen went to the neighboring town of Reutlingen to investigate the opinions of the local population about Böll's books in the belief that Böll would be popular in this working-class town. However, they found to their dismay that Böll's readers generally are not blue-collar workers, but white-collar workers interested in cultural and political events, and that they are more educated than the average German (Arbeitsgruppe 1975, 270). Böll is in fact an author for those circles where literature traditionally plays a leading role, the educated German middle class, a class whose post–World War II conscience he helped restore and define with his books.

Another important study of reaction to Heinrich Böll's work in Germany concentrates on his most controversial book, *The Lost Honor of Katharina Blum*. Anette Petersen lists various statistics of newspaper reviews about the book and summarizes Hans Habe's review of the novel as the most typical example of conservative criticism. Petersen reiterates that this was not a literary debate, but that it was dominated by political motives between Germany's Left and the Springer press (Petersen 1980).

Irene Charlotte Streul's study deals with the reception of West German literature in East Germany, where Böll's work played an important role. Streul summarizes general opinions in East Germany toward West German literature with good examples of the Böll reception in East Germany, and she relates GDR reviews to the political decisions in East German cultural politics (Streul 1988, 117–27).

The diligent work by Peter Bruhn and Henry Glade provides several well documented studies about Böll's popularity in the Soviet Union. Their first detailed analysis, which includes a bibliography of books by and about Böll in Russian, deals with the period from 1952 to 1979 (Bruhn/ Glade 1980). Other works dealing with Böll's reception in the Soviet Union include those by Martin Hüttel (Hüttel 1982) and another article by Glade, who informs us about the changed conditions in the Soviet Union under the auspices of Gorbachev's perestroika and the rehabilitation of Western writers, which included Heinrich Böll (Glade 1989).

There are also several studies concerning Böll's reception in Western countries outside West Germany. In 1968 the Swedish Germanist Gustav Korlén wrote his essay "Böll in Schweden" (Korlén 1968, 246). Korlén claims that in Sweden "the ideas of the Enlightenment never went out of style," and thus Erich Kästner's books are among the most popular in German literature. Korlén claims that Sweden, with its old social democratic traditions, was the ideal reception ground for Böll's enlightenment-inspired literature.

Erwin Theodor Rosenthal asserts that Böll's works have an international appeal because the conditions Böll describes are only superficially German, and that they in fact uncover social conditions of the entire Western world. Thus, Brazilians are enthusiastic readers of Böll's oeuvre (Rosenthal 1975).

Responses to Böll in the United States are much more complex than in any other country outside of West Germany. Ray Lewis White gave an excellent introduction into Böll's popular reception in America, with summaries of newspaper reviews from 1954 to 1970 (White 1979). Several other authors discuss the reluctant American reception of foreign literature; among them are Walter Ziltener (1982), who compares Böll's popularity with that of Günter Grass. Mark Rectanus uncovers the mechanism of the making of a best-seller (*The Lost Honor of Katharina Blum*) both in West Germany and the United States (Rectanus 1986). The situation in the United States is particularly difficult because there is a great difference between the reception-behavior of well-read academics and that of the general population. Rectanus states that no reviewer he analyzes attempted to relate the stories of Böll's books to political, social, or economic institutions in Germany, and that works of foreign literature are frequently reviewed in a "cultural vacuum" (Rectanus 1986, 266). Unlike in other countries, the general population in the United States seems little interested in finding out about the world and in relating their own social problems to those of the rest of the world. This situation is aggravated by the fact that many scholars working in the United States are concerned with German problems and are obviously interested in bridging the communication gap between academics and the general population.

Thomas Schaller discusses Böll's popularity in institutions of higher learning in the United States (Schaller 1988). He concludes that the perceived discrepancy between the work of Günter Grass and that of Heinrich Böll is not present among the academics he questioned for his survey. He also confirms the results of other studies that indicate that *Billiards at Half-Past Nine* was Böll's first big American success, not *The Clown*, as in Germany. Those two books are still the most popular ones among professors who teach German in America, whereas students normally choose *The Lost Honor of Katharina Blum* as their favorite Böll novel (Schaller 1988, 89).

The method of the present survey can be illustrated with an image taken from Böll's own work *The Lost Honor of Katharina Blum*, in which he describes the author's task as redirecting various streams so that they merge – his metaphor for the different sorts of information he is trying to merge into a readable text. This method works also in tracing critical reaction to Böll's oeuvre: the reception of Heinrich Böll's works can be divided into three independent bodies: the reception in the Marxist countries, in West Germany, and in other Western countries, especially Great Britain and the United States. Each of these fields will be treated separately because critics in these countries often relate almost exclusively to each other, as was especially true during the first phase of Böll scholarship from 1950 to 1968. Critics often refer only to other critics in their own field, and it seems as if Böll brought out cultural blinders, which readers and critics as members of their own respective cultures seem unable to overcome, be it an American reading Böll as a representative of an alien culture, a citizen of East Germany or the Soviet Union who sees Böll as a member of a capitalist society, a West German Marxist who sees Böll as a petit bourgeois, or a West German conservative who sees Böll as a subversive anarchist. In this maze, it was often impossible to find the author Heinrich Böll. Fortunately, however, a more comprehensive picture appeared by the 1980s, when large parts of the scholarship on Böll's work had merged into one general stream of writing. As part of the series *Literary Criticism in Perspective* the present survey shows how the surprising differences in reading Böll are mainly based in the reader's country of origin and his ideological perspective.

Böll's reception in West Germany is of course the key element in understanding the current status of this author. West German reception divides into two clearly defined periods: first in the heated political atmosphere lasting from 1968, which is marked by the beginning of the student revolts and the publication of Marcel Reich-Ranicki's *In Sachen Böll*, to 1978, a year when most major theoretical works about Böll appeared in Germany; second in the 1980s, in contrast a calmer period reflecting not only the end of Böll's creativity as a writer and his death but also the changed political atmosphere in West Germany after Helmut Kohl's "turnaround" (*Wende*) in 1982. Textual analyses became popular again, an approach which Anglo-American critics had continued to exercise during the 1970s while German academics were struggling with social theories.

The three geographic areas (the Marxist countries, the Anglo-American countries, and former West Germany) are discussed in three consecutive chapters, each chronologically. Ongoing themes are also identified, for example the debate surrounding *Group Portrait With Lady*, or the issues surrounding Böll's article on Ulrike Meinhof, and summarized in the chapter "Böll as a Political Writer." Since ongoing debates and arguments are often connected with a single literary critic, for example Hans Joachim Bernhard, the critical work of most authors has been kept together. With the above-mentioned exceptions, the chronological approach has been maintained throughout this survey. *Heinrich Böll: Forty Years of Criticism* aims mostly at exploring the academic reception of Heinrich Böll's work, and due to the wide scope of secondary sources only the most important material has been discussed. As many representative sources as possible have been included to give a overview over the trends in the reception.

I: MARXIST CRITICISM

A: Soviet Criticism

JUST AS THE SOVIET UNION dominated other Communist countries politically, Russian scholarship dictated its ideas to other Eastern European countries, especially during the 1950s and 1960s. As a result, Russian criticism of this period appears freer and more innovative than East German criticism, where critics were allowed only to follow established patterns of thinking that had originated in the Soviet Union. However, Böll was not introduced to the Soviet Union through official channels but was discovered by one of the most sensitive Böll critics anywhere, the Russian critic and professor of German, Lev Kopelev. In an article that Kopelev wrote for the German edition of the Russian literary journal *Soviet Literature* in 1957, four major points of interest for a Marxist reader of Böll's work are mentioned, all of them connected with the Russian admiration of the writer Fyodor Dostoyevsky (Kopelev 1957). In his comparison of Böll's work to that of Dostoyevsky, Kopelev is well aware of official reservations concerning the religious content of Böll's novels: (1) Kopelev praises Böll as an original realistic writer in Dostoyevsky's tradition; like Dostoyevsky, Böll "reinvented the art of storytelling"; (2) unlike Dostoyevsky, Böll does not preach or try to convince his readers of an eternal truth, an important difference counteracting Böll's obvious interest in religion; (3) Böll's characters are fighters, not pacifists or religious zealots who want to change the world as Dostoyevsky's characters are – a questionable interpretation of Böll's characters, but one necessary in the political climate of that place and time; (4) Böll's artistic achievements come from an Eastern European tradition of music, according to Kopelev, who observes that Böll's books are filled with "musical architecture" and dominated by a "minor key motif" ("Moll-Motiv"; Kopelev 1957, 152–57). Kopelev argues that Böll's literature should be immediately accessible to a Russian reader because of its artistic composition.

Kopelev was right; indeed, Böll became a major Western writer in the Soviet Union, second only to the American novelist Ernest Hemingway. However, on one count Kopelev misjudged the situation, since Böll appealed more to the intelligentsia than the Russian general public (Bruhn/Glade 1980, 56), a point that is supported by statistics from the Soviet periodical *Politicesky dnevnik* (Hüttel 1981, 98). A clear indication of general interest in Böll in the Soviet Union is the more than three hundred Russian articles about him listed in Glade and Bruhn's bibliography (see Glade 1982, 140). But Kopelev's argument concerning Böll's proximity to Dostoyevsky's way of thinking proved correct, since the two books closest to Dostoyevsky's world, *And Never Said a Word* and *The Bread of Those Early Years*, introduced Böll to the Soviet Union as a major literary figure (Glade 1989, 308). Soon Soviet literary criticism on Böll split into two camps, a conservative hard-line approach looking for political "strategies" in literature, and a more sensitive literature-centered approach that tried to capture the artistic achievements in Böll's work. The sensitive ("Romantic") approach is definitely represented by Kopelev's correlating musical themes with Böll's art, which could be compared to the discovery by the West German Klaus Jeziorkowski of the artistic rhythm in Böll's art. Similarly, the critic Irina Rodnyanskaya worked out "a mythical-poetic construction" for Böll's novels using a technique of parallel forms in space which enable the reader to comprehend the work in its intended simultaneousness and not as a temporal succession. Rodnyanskaya demonstrated with her text analysis that "Böll's work is often comprised of a hermetically sealed system similar to a musical system or a lyrical-epic composition" (Bruhn/Glade 1980, 32).

Among the hard-liners, however, Böll was regarded as a misguided member of the middle class who was unable to overcome his petit bourgeois limitations; thus, the Russian critic L. B. Cernaya pointed out the relationship between Böll's work and that of the Weimar writer Hans Fallada in a 1956 article in the Soviet literature periodical *Literaturnaya gazeta* with the provocative title "'Little Man' at Crossroads" (Bruhn/Glade 1980, 17). Böll's middle-class background was mentioned as a negative element by most orthodox reviewers. Most conservative reviewers preferred *The Unguarded House* to all other Böll novels of the 1950s. Therefore, this book soon acquired the status of Böll's best work among orthodox Marxists, since in the Bietenhahn chapter it presented a "utopian perspective." The East German critic Jürgen Kuczynski, who had received his initial training in Marxist party schools in the Soviet Union, was eager to promote hard-line Russian ideas in the GDR, and he picked up on Cernaya's portrayal of Böll's protagonists as precarious petit bourgeois characters typical of Fallada's works. The emerging East German literary criticism was never independent and would always follow the more orthodox trends in the Soviet Union. It was common for East German critics to follow their Russian masters in evaluating West German literature, since West Germany, as part of the capitalist system of the West, was considered a foreign literature by East Germans.

Böll's novel *Billiards at Half-Past Nine* divided the increasingly more liberal critics in the Soviet Union from the GDR hard-liners. While the critic I. Fradkin described this novel in his afterword of the Russian edition as "one of the greatest achievements of critical realism," picturing the "actual reality in the Federal Republic in its direct connection to the fascist militaristic past," most East German reviewers faulted Böll for his manner of using the "formalistic" stream-of-consciousness technique and for telling his novel from the viewpoint of his characters.

A major change in the Soviet Union came with the publication of Böll's *The Clown*. Established Soviet criticism discovered in this book a lack of "perspective" – which in Marxist language means a sense of dynamic progression in history (Bruhn/Glade 1980, 24). This impression that Böll's works offered a political perspective had played a major role in the acceptance of Böll's early books, above all of *The Unguarded House,* and for some reviewers it existed even in *Billiards.* However, no reviewer could discover such a progressive element in *The Clown*, and so the book demonstrated Böll's political "retrogression," a serious charge for Soviet critics. Although Böll's books continued to be appreciated for their radical criticism of Western values, a rift was developing between even the most forgiving Russian critics and Böll's political interests. Since the Soviet Union was not a member of the International Copyright Association at that time, Russian officials felt free to change the translation of *The Clown* by eliminating portions of the text, such as the undesirable Erfurt episode, where the clown Hans Schnier rejects East German party officials as narrow-minded. Perhaps because the Russian reading public had taken a great liking to Heinrich Böll's work, his

Gramley Library
Salem College
Winston-Salem, NC 27108

books could be rewritten but not banned. The Russian playwright G. L. Bortnikov rewrote and adapted *The Clown* into a play under the direction of B. Nord which was performed in Moscow for more than ten years and continued to be played even after Böll's books were no longer available in the Soviet Union.

Despite the growing irritation with Böll among official censorship authorities, *Group Portrait With Lady* was also published in the Soviet Union, although with considerable changes by the Germanist Cernaya, applying the Soviet censorship codex (Bruhn/Glade 1980, 41). Especially the episodes in Böll's novel that deal with the Soviet occupation of East Prussia seemed to have been a sore point, and everything that was remotely related to the Soviet intervention in Czechoslovakia was removed from the Russian text (Bruhn/Glade 1980, 47). It was furthermore impossible that a Soviet citizen, Leni's lover Boris, should be presented as a devout Christian; therefore, those passages that show Boris's Christianity were eliminated too (Hüttel 1981, 100). Thus, the text was seriously mutilated before it could be published in the Soviet Union. Since the moment the International Copyright Agreement was signed soon after this censorship case, no further cases of this magnitude have been reported from the Soviet Union. Despite the heavy censorship, however, most Soviet critics and readers were happy that the book was printed in their country and accepted it without reservation, as the Russian writer Konstantin Simonov, who in an interview with the East German author Christa Wolf called *Group Portrait With Lady* the best work Böll had ever written (Bruhn/Glade 1980, 49).

2. With the publication of *The Lost Honor of Katharina Blum*, however, the Soviet Union changed its official opinion about Böll, and in an official decree, the censorship agency Avtorskich prav (the Soviet Agency for Authors' Rights) announced that Böll had demanded an excessive amount of money for the publication rights of his book and that therefore the publication was not feasible – obviously a propaganda trick to justify withholding the novel from the Russian public. Thus, Böll's books were banned in the Soviet Union in 1974 despite their growing popularity. It was later admitted, however, that in fact the 1974 decree had stipulated a ban on Böll's work only in Russian, although it was still acceptable to publish his works in the languages

of other Soviet nationalities. The ambiguity of this order reflects the uneasiness officials felt in dealing with Böll as one of the most popular foreign authors in the Soviet Union. An anonymous reviewer, signing his name "Literator," in the influential *Literaturnaya gazeta*, the official organ of the Union of Soviet writers, justified the rejection of Böll's work in an article with the provocative title "Why Does the World Praise Heinrich Böll? On Heinrich Böll's Attacks on Soviet Literature" (Bruhn/Glade 1980, 55). The influential critic E. Knipovic supported the official charges leveled against Böll in the *Literaturnaya gazeta* and justified the ban on Böll's *The Lost Honor of Katharina Blum* for two reasons: (1) his attempt to make his protagonists "rise above the situation" would benefit the reactionaries, and (2) the connection between the all-powerful *News* (*Zeitung*) and the government's inability to protect Katharina is worked out only in a sketchy way (Bruhn/Glade 1980, 52). Such charges of inadequate political direction had already been aimed at Böll because of his earlier books, but they had not led to an overall ban. What Knipovic omits are the real motives behind the ban, namely Böll's support for Soviet dissidents such as Vladimir Bukovski and Andrey Amalrik, and above all his hospitality toward Alexander Solzhenitsyn in 1974 when Solzhenitsyn had to leave the Soviet Union.

Despite the official ban, Böll's work enjoyed a lasting popularity among the Russian people, since "the ironic coloring of his books and the intimate lyrical tone appealed to an astonishing number of Soviet prose writers," especially among liberals and dissidents, who discovered a congruence between Böll's experience of life and their own (Bruhn/Glade 1980, 57). Ironically, Böll's work benefited from the withdrawal of official favor, and in the seventies he became an author widely published by underground (samizdat) presses. Böll's short stories became his most popular works in the Soviet Union, in which the Russian reader understands Böll's antiheroes as the "type of the gray, anonymous white-collar worker, behind whom lurks Kafka's semi-anonymous K-type" (Glade 1982, 141).[1] Böll's Russian readers clearly recognized his subversive intentions, which helped them to

---

[1] Glade quotes Klaus Jeziorkowski's monograph *Rhythmus und Figur*, in which many of Böll's heroes or anti-heroes, e.g., in "Der Lacher" or "Es wird etwas geschehen," "den Typ des grauen, namenlosen Angestellten verkörpern, hinter dem (. . .) der halbanonyme K.-Typ Kafkas zu stehen scheint."

understand their own alienated situation. The West German Marxist Martin Hüttel explained Böll's appeal in the Soviet Union by noting that Böll's political ambivalence made it possible for both reader groups in the Soviet Union, the liberals and the conservatives alike, to adopt Böll for their respective ideologies (Hüttel 1981, 107). Again, Böll's humanist pacifism convinced the Soviet authorities to allow the publication of an excerpt from *Das Vermächtnis* in *Literaturnaja gazeta* in its January 5, 1983, issue (Glade 1985, 74).

With the rise of perestroika, Böll's work was once again published in the Soviet Union, and a "Böll renaissance" or "Böll rehabilitation" began with the most complete edition of his collected works ever. Once again Russian publishers changed the translated text without consultation, as in the first publication of *The Lost Honor of Katharina Blum*, where sexual expressions like "bumsen" were eliminated (Glade, Mayer 1989). The 1989 edition of Böll's work with more than 200,000 copies demonstrates his popularity clearly in comparison with the complete printed work of Anna Seghers (75,000 copies) and that of Bertolt Brecht (12,500 copies). These figures express the gratitude that an entire generation of Russian writers felt toward Heinrich Böll, who through his subversive strategies and his unorthodox, idealistic thinking helped them overcome their dependence on rigid socialism.

With the demise of Marxism in virtually every Eastern European country, it is now China that still clings to the same values the Soviets aspired to for the past thirty years in regard to Böll. Ni Cheng'en (1992) asserts that Böll enjoys the same high reputation in China as he did in the Soviet Union. In China, Böll and Hemingway are the two most important foreign authors. Cheng'en, however, brings a new twist into the discussion when she emphasizes the Chinese interest in Böll's aesthetic values and claims he is so popular in China, "because his works are traditional and at the same time avant-garde" (Cheng'en 1992, 313). It may just be that she wants China not to appear backwards in front of the trend toward more experimental forms.

It would be appropriate to conclude this brief chapter on Böll's reception in the Soviet Union and China with a return to comments by Lev Kopelev, Böll's Russian friend who facilitated his first lecture trip to the Soviet Union in 1962. Later Kopelev became yet another Soviet dissident who left and subsequently moved to Cologne, and as a close friend gave the eulogy at Böll's funeral in 1985. In an earlier essay

Kopelev had summarized why people all over the world love Böll's books; he was a writer convinced that "ethics and aesthetics cannot be separated, . . . and that his conscience is his moral and aesthetic category" (Kopelev 1976, 68). According to Kopelev, this rare organic unity in a body of literature makes Böll one of the greatest writers of all time.

B: East German Criticism

1. Irene Charlotte Streul states that East Germany's reception of Heinrich Böll's work began in 1960, when the influential GDR critic Hans-Jürgen Geerdts praised Böll as the only Western writer who adhered to "critical realism," the Western version of socialist realism officially sanctioned by GDR cultural politicians. Geerdt's appraisal of Böll's style was in fact an official endorsement, and subsequently Böll became through his novels a major spokesman for the Federal Republic in Eastern European countries (Streul 1988, 59). The final endorsement came in 1961 during the Fifth Party Congress from the acclaimed socialist writer Anna Seghers, who criticized all Western writers as too schematic and repetitious – with the exception of Heinrich Böll.

Frank Wagner was one of the first GDR literary critics to provide a thorough discussion of Böll's work from a Marxist perspective. Wagner notes as positive in Böll's work his interest in the working class, and he further notes Böll's insistence on discussing topics concerned with the resurgence of old Nazis. However, Wagner faults Böll for his inability to rise above his characters to show his readers a way out of their capitalist misery. Since Böll himself is unable to recognize the truth, he can only show life in obscure literary symbols as he did in *Billiards at Half-Past Nine* (Wagner 1961, 122).

East German criticism approached the work of the most popular West German author very cautiously over the next ten years. Jürgen Kuczynski, the patriarch of East Germany's Marxist sociology, complained in 1962 that Fred Bogner in *And Never Said a Word* reminded him of the religious sculptures of the artist Ernst Barlach in their complacency. As a Marxist who had experienced Weimar society firsthand, Kuczynski believed that Barlach, and with him the entire expressionist art movement, was responsible for Hitler's rise, a theory Marxists had established in the "expressionism-debate" during the 1930s. Communists were quick to denounce anybody as petit bourgeois (*Kleinbürger*) who did not fit their ideological mold, as all non-Marxist artists before and after 1933. Kuczynski ironically portrays Fred Bogner, who returned to his wife and his family in *And Never Said a Word*, as someone who just goes home and thereby resigns himself to political inaction out of confused incompetence (Kuczynski 1962). Kuczynski was not satisfied to assault the politically confused expressionist movement of the Weimar Republic; he intended a further blow against Böll's art with an allusion to the perhaps best-known writer of the Weimar Republic, Hans Fallada, and his portrayal of "little people." With his novel *Little Man – What Now?*, Fallada had introduced a term into political terminology in 1932 with the connotation that the small worker and employee, a mere victim of social changes, was unable to change the course of society. Kuczynski, however, was merely echoing an allegation made about Fallada by the West German news-magazine *Der Spiegel* in 1961, which had labeled Böll a Catholic Fallada (*Der Spiegel* 1961, 71–86).

Hermann Kant was the first to describe Böll as a modern writer and pointed to Böll's Western style as a model, thereby separating himself from the Communist dogma that modernism equaled decadence. Kant accepted the possibility that Böll's critical realism was aesthetically innovative and accepted it as a fair representation of social conditions, which traditionally had been the domain of socialist realism (Streul 1988, 122).

Horst Haase took Kant's lead and tried to explain the symbolism in *Billiards at Half-Past Nine* as an expression for Böll's search "for the meaning of the history of our people in the twentieth century" ("[der] Sinn der Geschichte unseres Volkes"; Haase 1964, 226) but rejected Böll's choice of symbols as too simplistic, as did most other Marxists. And from his orthodox Marxist perspective, Haase argues that the representatives of Böll's lamb symbol come from the "proletarian or plebeian sphere," which the middle-class setting of the novel proves false. The buffalo symbol is criticized for its inability to grasp "the complexities of the economic roots of the symbolized forces," since members of the buffalo caste are perceived as too powerful (Haase 1964, 225). And in order to argue against Böll's symbolic dichotomy, the Marxist Haase claims that the inequality of strong buffaloes versus meek lambs completely misrepresented the power structure. He argues that the lower classes would have only had to collect their real strength in order to shed the yoke of Nazi domination, whereas Böll's symbol suggests a much stronger power base of the Nazis and the traditional ruling classes in German society.

Günter Jäckel continued Haase's criticism of Böll's symbols for their being taken from the sphere of nature and described *Billiards at Half-Past Nine* as a form of domesticating nature. Böll has, according to Jäckel, a tendency to exclude nature from his fiction and to use nature only in certain images to illustrate his viewpoint. In his instrumental use of nature, Böll shows a hierarchical image of nature, where everybody knows his place and works in an almost idyllic way under the patriarch (Jäckel 1968, 1289). By analyzing Böll's use of nature as a metaphor, Jäckel demonstrates Böll's lack of ideological understanding of West German society.

As in the Soviet Union, East German criticism became more divided with the publication of *The Clown*. Klaus Hermsdorf, for example, who has obviously read Jeziorkowsky's West German newspaper reviews with their existential phraseology about Böll, attacks Böll's belief in nihilism ("Bekenntnis zum Nichts") as a completely inappropriate stance for a realistic writer (Hermsdorf 1964, according to Streul 1988, 94). Likewise, Günter Cwojdrak maintains that *The Clown* is the author's capitulation to West German society, "a tearful complaint" without any direction (Streul 1988, 95).

Kurt Batt's thesis seems to be that although Böll is a progressive author, he never was and never will be able to develop his progressive ideas under the existing repressive circumstances in West Germany. Therefore, Böll will not rise above the confused perspective of his fictional characters in *The Unguarded House*. Batt, one of the main ideologues of East German literary criticism, demonstrates in this verdict the tightening of East Germany's official policy toward Böll, since it had been this book that most Marxists had praised earlier as an accurate portrayal of West German society (Batt 1974). Also, Batt maintains that Böll shows a typical petit bourgeois moralistic bitterness toward the rulers of capitalist society in *The Clown*. Batt claims Böll's hatred of "fascistoid" restoration in West Germany produces nothing but literary caricatures like the clown Schnier himself or allegorical signs that are difficult to decode, as in *Billiards at Half-past Nine*. Since Böll is completely blind toward existing power conditions, Batt claims, Böll clings in his confusion to a "rudimentary ideal of a petty bourgeois democracy" that "burns under the ashes of disappointments and bitterness" (Batt 1974, 151). Obviously, Batt has no desire to separate the author's intention from that of his poetic figures, a deliberate confusion that was soon to spread to other Marxist critics in East *and* West Germany. The identity of the author's intention with the aims of the fictional characters was one of the characteristics of primitive socialist realism. Thus Batt claims that Böll's intended social criticism fails and produces cheap petit bourgeois family novels that are not worth reading – pulp. Batt sees Böll mainly as a social critic who gets scared of his own courage and is content to offer a solution of a "simple life" in a cozy home. However, Batt still praises *The Clown* as Böll's best attempt to reject his own capitalist society, because the author Böll (being identical with the protagonist Schnier) distances himself from his own petit bourgeois background through this novel. East German critics such as Batt still saw hope that Böll would develop into a real Marxist.

2. This hope was discussed in more detail in the first book-length study of Böll, by Günter Wirth. Rainer Nägele calls Wirth's approach "a mixture of conservative theology with socialist vocabulary" and without a stringent ideological concept. Wirth is fascinated by Böll's work and calls him "a Christian humanist" (Wirth 1967, 216) in the best Lukácsian tradition and a writer whose work is "understood" in the German Democratic Republic (Wirth 1967, 223). But as Nägele stated, besides some conservative Christian rhetoric, Wirth's book only rephrases common East German judgments of Böll's work, when he criticizes *Adam, Where Art Thou?* for its limited social perspective or when he notices a "pagan existentialism" in the primeval experience of anxiety in *The Train Was On Time* (Wirth 1967, 54). Wirth points out more directly that Böll attacked bureaucratic tendencies in the German clergy in *Billiards at Half-Past Nine* as the main obstacle to decent human development. In Wirth's criticism of *The Unguarded House*, his notion of "humanness" or everyday Christianity becomes clearer; he calls it the "life that could have been but did not materialize" (Wirth 1967, 120). Wirth's efforts at combining socialism

with Christianity are worked out even more in his discussion of the "progressive Catholic citizen" embodied in the protagonist Albert in *The Bread of Those Early Years* and in Robert Fähmel in *Billiards at Half-Past Nine* .

All of Böll's characters represent something that Wirth calls social humanism, a summary of what he sees as the most progressive elements of the German bourgeoisie. With this humanism, Wirth claims, Böll continues the best German humanist traditions as they are expressed in Thomas Mann's work. By combining worldly humanism with his religious themes, according to Wirth, Böll begins a new literary tradition; he is a progressive writer working toward Catholic renovation. Thus it becomes obvious that Wirth recognizes Böll's liberal Catholicism as a progressive political force. Wirth combines orthodox Marxist vocabulary with his perceptive interpretation of Böll's Christianity. His difficulty, however, is in trying to popularize religion, which even when labeled a progressive element still would not find official Communist Party approval.

A further device Wirth uses to distance Böll from East German society is his attempt to show Böll as a regional writer for West Germany and the Cologne district, in order to mute possible notions of political reference to the GDR system. And in fact, Böll himself apparently does just that in his portrayal of Ireland in *The Irish Journal*, in which he describes Irish and German conditions as being diametrically opposed to each other. Wirth faults Böll for his socially damaging and unrealistic remarks about Irish society, remarks such as "Europe's social order took a different shape," or "poverty was no longer a shame," and "it was neither honor nor shame: it was as irrelevant as wealth." These statements are dangerous, according to Wirth, since Böll sees Ireland's social order in an unrealistic, romantic light by taking it out of the historical flow of social development (Wirth 1967, 220).[1] There are, however, some ironic parallels between

---

[1] "Denn wenn Böll bereits auf der ersten Seite dieses Tagebuchs schreibt, daß schon auf dem Deck des Dampfers, der ihn nach Irland führt, 'Europas soziale Ordnung andere Formen' annahm und Armut , 'nicht nur keine Schande' mehr war, sondern, weder Ehre noch Schande: sie war – als Moment gesellschaftlichen Selbstbewußtseins – 'so belanglos wie Reichtum', so wird doch durch eine solche Stellungnahme der Zustand der gesellschaftlichen Ordnung in Irland aus dem geschichtlichen Fluß, aus der gesellschaftlichen Entwicklung herausgenommen, isoliert und letzten Endes glorifiziert."

Böll's and Wirth's perceptions of the Irish society; whereas Wirth regards his own society as a realized and totally rationalized utopia according to Marx's views, Böll considers Ireland a real alternative to Germany, although as a historically grown society it is completely irrational – a religious irrationality Böll considered essential for a living society. The fundamental difference between Böll and East German society remained: East Germany could not allow any criticism of its society, whereas Böll's prime interest lay in criticizing his own society.

3. Serious East German scholarship on Heinrich Böll did not begin until Hans Joachim Bernhard's book, in which he portrayed Böll as West Germany's most important prose writer (Bernhard 1970, 7). With this book, Bernhard established himself single-handedly as probably the most important Böll expert not just in the GDR but also in West Germany, because he soon had considerable impact on the emerging Marxists in West Germany. Nägele compared the importance of Bernhard's book to that of the West German Durzak: "The nearest thing to a dialectical examination of form and content is the studies by Manfred Durzak and Hans Joachim Bernhard" (Nägele, "Aspects," 1976, 65). Nägele's only objection is that Bernhard's method is still too conventional in its reliance on formalistic approaches. Irene Streul characterizes Bernhard's approach as an attempt to combine social criticism with a support for Böll's utopian visions, not as a dichotomy but as a dialectical interchange, since Bernhard believes in the "reflection character" (*Abbildcharacter*) of literature (Streul 1988, 124).

In his book Bernhard provides good examples of dialectical interchange in Böll's work in several detailed analyses of his early novels and short stories. Bernhard maintains, for example, that the story "Traveler, if you Come to Spa . . ." allows the reader to recognize the cause of evil through the story's open form and especially its open end. Similarly, Bernhard maintains, the novel *The Train Was on Time* allows for a creative reader much as a detective novel does through the text's having a very clear and linear structure; the "linearity" of the narrative structure reflects the simple dimensionality of death in war. According to Bernhard, Böll's intention in his first texts was to show "with epic means an impressive picture of the functioning of the system into which the individual is forced" (Bernhard 1970, 49). Like other Marxist critics before him, Bernhard criticizes Böll's inability to uncover the causes of war, especially in the novel *Adam, Where Art Thou?*, when Bernhard remarks that the really guilty ones and the social powers that led to the war do not appear in this book (54). However, Bernhard defends Böll's use of disease as a metaphor for war since it takes an extraordinary and irrational symbol to convey an appropriate impression of the powers of war.[1]

Although he likes the portrayal of Nella in *The Unguarded House*, he argues that her spontaneous protest changes only her private life, not the social conditions. Bernhard criticizes *The Unguarded House* as showing the West German restoration as too powerful, since the only remedy is in a limited geographic area, the peaceful town of Bietenhahn; in this, Bernhard comes close to Kurt Batt's critical view. Bernhard describes the Bietenhahn episode as an attempt to create an ideal world comparable to Böll's perspective on Ireland (in *The Irish Journal*), a utopian and unrealistic view.

Bernhard praises Böll's excellent choice of symbolism in *The Bread of Those Early Years*, "since it uncovers the power of money that permeates all human behavior" (133), much as Durzak in West Germany reacted. Therefore, Bernhard maintains, the quality of Böll's work is in his clearly defined image-symbols that condense the scope of the shown reality to a clearer picture; these symbols let his work stand out above all other realistic West German literature.

Bernhard's discussion of *Billiards at Half-Past Nine* demonstrates well his perception of Böll's method. Bernhard praises the book primarily because of Böll's "limitation technique" of capturing the broadest possible spectrum of German history. In his dialectical method of understanding the novel, Bernhard uses Heinrich Strautmann's thesis that "coming to terms with the complexity of the time problem is a phenomenon of our century" ("das 'Gewahrwerden der Komplexität des Zeitproblems'"; Bernhard 1970, 227). Since the book focuses on methods of condensing our perception of time, Bernhard argues that Böll's techniques are not formalistic games, as so often with other Western writers, who in their own limited understanding of reality are unable to give us a clear picture of reality. Böll,

---

[1] The West German critic Konrad Kurz came to the same positive conclusion about the symbol of disease (Bernhard 1970, 22).

according to Bernhard, shows with his technique that the destruction of time in reality parallels the destruction of reality in society – a fragmented reality requires a fragmented literary representation. However, Böll does not stop at the simple depiction of capitalist reality, as Bernhard points out; his viewpoint goes beyond that of the suffering individuals in his novels, whose rights he defends against the powers of history. Thus Bernhard claims (unlike Batt) that Böll has indeed a proper progressive perception of history, and only at some points does he lack artistic skills to represent these forces properly in his fiction. Therefore, Böll is definitely an author recommended for general reading in the GDR.

In discussing *The Clown*, Bernhard denounces Western critics who had begun to label Böll's work according to formal criteria such as "standard" or "modern" and who completely disregarded the author's ideological position. Bernhard argues that these denunciations are intended only to discredit any humanistic author like Böll since such writers disrupt the antihumanist consensus of West German society. Bernhard's perception is obviously wrong, since Western critics had indeed shown a great deal of appreciation for *Billiards at Half-Past Nine*; it was with the publication of *The Clown* that a majority of Western critics began to question Böll's artistic ability.

Thus Bernhard's argument is mainly a defense of *The Clown*, which although it lacks the skillful, artistic devices of *Billiards*, shows more than the earlier book "a sharpness in attack" ("eine Schärfe des Angriffs"; Bernhard 1970, 301). With this book and its moral engagement, Bernhard claims, Böll found his very own literary form, which anticipates the political battles and books to come. Bernhard interprets the book as a general accounting of West Germany's failures whose poignancy is achieved through its utmost subjectivity. Despite this straightforward praise, Bernhard objects to Böll's presentation of Schnier as a member of the upper middle class, which makes him less believable when he attacks society. Bernhard, like other Marxists, would have liked to see a member of the working class carry the book's protest – again a gross misperception of existing social conditions in West Germany. The students who revolted only a few years later were all sons and daughters of the affluent middle classes. The conflict, however, goes much deeper, as East German officials deplored the real student revolts later, and as these revolts indeed represented a serious threat to the East German political system.

In 1972 Bernhard wrote a review article about *Group Portrait With Lady*; Böll's novel had been published two years after Bernhard's book. Bernhard continues his method of combining a structural and symbol analysis with a discussion of Böll's political intentions and concludes that *Group Portrait With Lady* grew organically out of Böll's previous work, as there is "hardly a motif in Böll's work that is not worked into Leni's life story" (Bernhard 1972, 272). He further praises Leni as an embodiment of Böll's humanistic image of man, assembling in her person a model of resistance to antihuman trends in society. Bernhard continues to see Böll's idealistic characters as models of a socialist well-rounded person, along with a possibility that the author might someday see things the same way East German Communists did. However, Bernhard faults Böll's representation of Leni as an ideal too far removed from the current social conditions in West Germany and, consistent with his method, finds this faulty idealism reflected in the book's narrative structure. At the end of the novel, a break in the narrator's report occurs when the narrator, who remains neutral up to that point, becomes more and more involved in Leni's affairs and offers his personal opinion. The break, Bernhard argues, hides a basic ideological concept in Böll's writing, which in turn represents the basic flaw in capitalist society that does not allow even a progressive writer like Böll to understand his society's problems (274).

In another essay Bernhard continued his discussion of Leni as the embodiment of every humanistic value Böll had presented in his literature up to that point. Now Bernhard's defense of Böll's traditional mode of narrative technique sounds more desperate, since both Böll and the "traditional" narrative technique in the GDR, socialist realism, have to defend their position. Thus Bernhard argues that Böll hangs on to his writing style "despite the turmoil in the literary market and its fashions." As a steady writer Böll could not be made nervous by the hectic atmosphere of the 1960s (Bernhard, "Gruppenbild mit Dame" 1975, 61). This statement is further evidence of Bernhard's cautious attitude toward experiments in literature and the social experiments during West Germany's student revolts. Again, external social conditions are reflected in Leni as a symbolic focal point; she is vulnerable on the inside but indestructible on the outside, thereby demonstrating the invincibility of Böll's belief in humanity in the inhumane capitalist world. Leni as a character and as a symbol, Bernhard claims, is thus the highest possible "poetic manifestation of a human existence ... even in a capitalist society," (". . . poetische Manifestierung einer humanen Existenz auch . . . in der 'Profitgesellschaft'"; Bernhard 1975, 63). *Group Portrait With Lady* above all is the reason for Böll's international reputation, according to Bernhard. Leni is the epitomy of Böll's art.

In another essay Bernhard traces Böll's writing to humanistic traditions of the pre-World War II era, especially to those of Thomas Mann, whose protagonist Tonio Kröger in the novella with the same name is as vulnerable and sensitive as Leni (Bernhard, "Grundpositionen" 1975). The writer Tonio Kröger observes bourgeois behavior and develops his own concept to stay away from the bourgeoisie. Just as the model-character Kröger embodies all the sensitivities of his time and thereby epitomizes its potential, Leni represents in Bernhard's interpretation all the sensitive potential of her time. The critic Bernd Kügler attacked Bernhard's Marxist viewpoint as no longer related to the social base of the literature he should be discussing. Kügler reasons that human behavior does not originate on the level of ideological and academic discussion, but from the authentic representation of experienced time (Kügler 1982, 426).

In a later essay, Bernhard offered a more reserved evaluation of Böll, a sort of "self-criticism," and distanced himself from his earlier theory of the absolute unity of Böll's work, stating that "his moral position became blinded to reality" and thus allowed him to attack socialism. After the decision in the 1970s to drop Böll from the list of favored authors in the GDR, Bernhard needed to change his opinion about Böll again and offered an even more reserved evaluation of the author (Streul 1988, 127).

4. East German officials felt increasingly uneasy about Böll's political and literary activities, and in the early 1970s a ban of his books was discussed, as it had been in the Soviet Union. In 1970 a decision was made to drop Böll from the list of favored authors in the GDR; however, this did not mean a total ban of his work. Böll continued to be published in East Germany, where all of his newer books were

released except for *Group Portrait With Lady* (Streul 1988, 190–91). However, Marxist ideas had now passed on to West German intellectuals, and established critics like Bernhard and Wirth were still allowed to write about Böll, although with a more orthodox Marxist approach. Kurt Batt continued his critical assessment of contemporary West German literature, and in a collection of essays he defined West Germany's more advanced writers such as Böll as "internal rebels" (Batt 1974). Batt signals a continued GDR partiality toward Böll's way of writing by his maintaining that Böll is not a modernist writer as compared with the ex-East German writer Uwe Johnson. Böll, Batt claims, has found his unique realistic writing style and avoids the current crisis of fiction. Batt questions "whether current art forms have not come to their end and whether they should not be replaced with antiart," echoing tenets of the protesting student generation. Batt asks in the aftermath of the student revolts and after the publication of Böll's *End of a Mission* whether art in the West is identical with political action or whether political action can already be an aesthetic event which renders art redundant (Batt 1974, 6) – obviously questions that no writer in the GDR ever had to ask himself. Thus by pointing to the crucial question of Böll's political engagement through his literature, Batt deliberately highlights the differences between the political systems.

In his evaluation of Böll's *Group Portrait With Lady*, a novel not published in the GDR, Batt credits Böll with a revolutionary sensibility and a good understanding of the living conditions of his petit bourgeois heroes, the little people. What becomes apparent in this review is Batt's ideological embrace of an author whose book could not be purchased in the GDR. Batt obviously signals his readiness to accept the author again as a proper spokesman for West German society. However, Batt might have regretted his earlier attacks and hoped that perhaps both the GDR officials and Böll would give in somewhat. Böll's opus, Batt continues, is a unique occurrence in West German intellectual life and shows "that an author based in a democratic-humanistic position . . . can understand our basic problems much more critically than most of those impatient rebels with their revolutionary attitudes who reject our entire traditional literature as 'bourgeois' and who proclaim its death" (41).[1] Batt's notion of the missed opportunity becomes very clear here in his argument that he and Böll are contemporaries, who, although living in two different countries and social systems, should work together to protect the humanist heritage against the hordes of angry young men set to destroy humanist values and the entire social tradition. It seems as if Batt anticipated in his essay the ultimate failure of GDR officials in reaching out to the younger generation.

As mentioned earlier, Wirth also continued to denounce Böll's work. Two of Wirth's essays were included (as was one by Bernhard) in a 1975 volume on Böll published by the Australian Germanist Manfred Jurgensen, an indication of Wirth's increasing popularity outside Germany. The first article deals with *The Lost Honor of Katharina Blum*, and due to his interest in religious symbols, Wirth sees Katharina as an incarnation of the Saint Catharine symbol whose iconographic elements and legend comprise the structural elements of the novel (Wirth, "Plädoyer," 1975, 107). Again, Wirth uses a combination of a traditional symbol analysis combined with standard Marxist vocabulary when he claims that the novel shows a "serious crisis of the capitalist society" and uncovers "the capitalist power that comes from the banks and the power centers of psychological warfare" (Wirth, "Plädoyer," 1975, 97).[2]

Although Wirth's second essay of 1975 shows an equally hard-line approach in using the officially endorsed language, it nevertheless presents a degree of innovation. Wirth analyzes in his essay Böll's "Epilog zu Stifters *Nachsommer*" and focuses on the key symbol, the *cereus peruvianus* (a flower) that embodies the protagonist Heinrich Drendorf's artificial world of petty Biedermeier traditions. Although

---

[1] "Die langsame Entfaltung von Bölls Oeuvre, das fraglos unter den derzeitigen Bedingungen in der BRD eine Rarität ist, lehrt zudem, daß ein Autor, der von einer demokratisch-humanistischen Grundposition ausgeht und die politischen und kulturellen Vorgänge kritisch beteiligt verfolgt, die Lebensprobleme weitaus genauer zu erfassen vermag als die meisten jener ungeduldigen Rebellen, die mit revolutionären Attitüden auftrumpfen, die überkommene Literatur insgesamt als bürgerlich diffamieren und deren Ende proklamieren."

[2] "Die verlorene Ehre der Katharina Blum - das ist keine romantische Verklärung anarchistischer Gewalt, das ist vielmehr die Aufdeckung jener Gewalt in der kapitalistischen Gesellschaft, die von den Banktresoren und den Zentralen der psychologischen Kriegsführung ausgeht."

Drendorf believes reality exists only in nature, the scene where Natalie puts the flower in her hair to seduce him demonstrates the impossibility of introducing nature into the settled bourgeois way of life. Thus Drendorf has to settle for a porcelain flower for his family (in a protective case). Wirth parallels this flower with the current situation in West Germany, where revanchism is on the rise, and reactionaries try to reinterpret Stifter's work for their own purposes. Although Wirth does not intend to criticize Böll's work with his accusation, he still maintains that Böll misunderstands Stifter, since Böll is not a nature writer. However, Wirth excuses Böll's failure to imitate Stifter, since a nature writer like Stifter could not be treated in any manner other than making him "artificial" (*verkünstelnd*) (Wirth, "Tradition," 1975, 137). In the end, Wirth refutes Stifter in order to save Böll.

In a 1979 essay Wirth offers a general settling of accounts (*General-abrechnung*) with Böll, in which he summarizes East German reservations concerning Böll's writing. Wirth asks whether he and other Marxists had not misjudged Böll earlier by putting too much emphasis on statements in which Böll had expressed criticism of the Federal Republic. Wirth criticizes himself and other Marxists for having ignored several of Böll's allegations against socialism, since they had all along believed in his potential development toward socialism and hoped to have Böll as a participant in an imaginary people's front movement. Wirth cites several interviews in which Böll "refused to criticize West German refugee politics" and showed open revanchism (Wirth 1979, 69). Böll, Wirth continues, does not understand that there is no other "Western European country where due to . . . ideological indoctrination the traditions and organizational forms of a democratic and humanistic bourgeoisie have been destroyed to the extent as in the Federal Republic" (Wirth 1979, 66).[1] Although these conditions make it hard for an average citizen to understand the amount of ideological disguise that surrounds him, a writer, especially a political writer, should be able to see through this disguise. Wirth cites prominent intellectuals like Niemöller and Rossaint who were able to

---

[1] ". . . daß es keinen anderen westeuropäischen Staat gibt, in dem im Gefolge der sozialen Entwicklung und der ideologischen Indoktrination die Traditionen und Organisationsformen eines demokratischen und humanistischen Bürgertums so zersetzt worden sind wie in der BRD."

see through the cover-up, while Böll "proceeded to a position which, considering world historical laws, must be regarded as one of provincialism in late bourgeois society already shaken by crises" (70).[1] This lack of a defined political position is reflected in Böll's political essays, as Wirth claims. Böll, in other words, "is no Thomas Mann, or Heinrich Mann or Arnold Zweig" – all authors whose perceptions of the political movements and social conditions clearly surpasses Böll's confused perspective.

In 1988 Wirth offered his final assessment of Böll in a critical review of *Women in a River Landscape* The topic Böll chose for his novel appeals to Wirth, since it connects once again with the issue of Christianity, which Böll "offers as a secular dimension" (Wirth 1988, 449).[2] Symbols abound, both Christian and non-Christian; an unrepented concentration camp crime, profits falsely justified – topics typical of Böll and, as we now understand, also typical of Wirth. Thus Wirth comes to his conclusion that "*Women in a River Landscape . . .* has the character of the turn about [*Wende*]" (Wirth 1988, 443). The term is Chancellor Helmut Kohl's word for his conservative "revolution" in 1982 upon assuming the chancellorship from Helmut Schmidt. Wirth sees the book as a typical product of this *Wende*, i.e., as "abuse of Christianity," since the West German conservatives were not interested in improving their country's moral status; instead, they wanted to improve the market to maximize profits. Böll knew all that very well but was too weak to resist in a form other than his last novel Adenauer's self-proclaimed "grandson," Helmut Kohl.

Wirth, in his reviews, sympathized more and more with Heinrich Böll's Christianity, a strange interest for the former GDR, but it seems fitting for this critic, who saw the GDR as a moral institution that had taken over Christian morality. Wirth thereby reflects the entire spectrum of Marxist responses to a successful West German writer.

[1] ". . . die subjektive Verantwortlichkeit eines Dichters, der weltliterarischen Anspruch hat und Moralist ist."

[2] "Und Böll wäre nicht Böll geblieben, würde er es nicht verstanden haben, auch in seinem letzten Roman die religiöse Dimension als weltliche darzubieten ... ."

II: AMERICAN CRITICISM

A: Introducing Heinrich Böll

THE RECEPTION OF HEINRICH BÖLL'S WORK in the United States is a history of frustrations and misunderstandings, mirroring the difficult overall relationship between the United States and Germany. Superficially, the countries subscribe to a philosophy of close friendship, but as soon as more specific intellectual and literary questions are raised, large areas of disagreement surface. In order to understand the conditions for limited reception of German literature and specifically for Heinrich Böll's work in the United States, we need to look at the conditions for intellectual exchange between the two countries. The general situation in the United States concerning the reception of foreign literature is puzzling, to say the least, and of great concern to teachers and publishers of foreign languages and literature alike. It is very rare that a French, Spanish, or German book makes the bestseller lists in the United States, unlike in other Western countries, including England and those in South America. Since only best-sellers are published and promoted with the help of major critics, there are few translations of German books available in America (Ziltener 1982, 3). Of the approximately 21,000 new books in Germany each year, about 750 (3.5 percent) are published in the United States, and of those only about thirty (0.1 percent) are reviewed annually in the *New York Times*, the foremost trendsetter in establishing literary criteria, as Volkmar Sander found in a statistical survey (Sander 1976, 163). Horst Daemmrich echoes this concern with his criticism of the careless attitude Americans have taken toward educating their children about foreign languages and cultures; the American mind, Daemmrich writes, "refers in an isolationistic manner back to itself" ("... ist der amerikanische Geist noch immer isolationistisch auf sich bezogen"; Daemmrich 1969, 319). Sander quotes a French critic stating that the French were beginning to understand that with prominent writers like Thomas Mann, Brecht, Benn, Musil, Broch, and Döblin, German literature was perhaps the most important literature of our century (Sander 1976, 172). However, Sander observes that it would be unimaginable for an American critic to write such a sentence and deduces that there is a general sense of cultural egocentrism in the United States.

Frank Trommler offers an insightful theory of intellectual and literary relations between the Old and the New World when he notes that American students can "read" and understand a text often much better than their European counterparts, since the text-based methods of the New Critical school had never completely disappeared in America. The current poststructural and deconstructionist methods are proof of the popularity of a text-based analysis, which the Germans denounced in the 1960s and 1970s as bourgeois. Trommler approaches the antagonism between text-based analyses in the United States and sociological approaches to literature in Germany from a historical viewpoint (Trommler 1979, 246-55). He shows how in the United States the concept of personal privacy developed in the nineteenth century and how it differed from that in German or French culture. Trommler relates the American idea of privacy to the early experience of the American frontier, where the individual had to create his own space out of wilderness. Similarly, the reader, Trommler argues, is alone with the text and by the act of reading establishes his relationship with it; he creates a private intellectual space away from other readers. In Europe, however, space had always been at a premium and could only be carved out from other existing spaces; it is considered a historical entity. Therefore, literature in Europe could and can only be read and understood in its distinct context, both historical and contemporary.

This may explain why in Europe, and especially in Germany, those writers who are concerned with historical and contemporary social conditions are the most popular. Since knowledge of the social and historical background is assumed and necessary for an educated person, it is obvious that the writers to whom Germans are attracted the most are also the most difficult to understand outside their original cultural context. The "context-loaded" texts that are popular in Germany are usually not well received in the United States. The reverse has also been true, at least since the 1960s; "context-free" texts are not popular in Germany, although this situation changed somewhat in the 1980s with increased interest in texts by postmodern authors like Botho Strauss and Thomas Bernhard.

Jeffrey Sammons put the blame for the unpopularity of German literature in the United States on those professors of German literature in America who had abandoned their own American critical traditions for the sake of German ones (Sammons 1977, 114). Sammons argued against such uncritical replacement of literary methods, since Americans do not have the sociological background in literary criticism that Germans have had since the late 1960s (Sammons 1978). Volkmar Sander deplores the fact that of the important works of the 1960s by German social theorists, only Ludwig Marcuse's books were translated, and other important philosophers such as Max Horkheimer, Theodor Adorno, Leo Löwenthal, and Jürgen Habermas were ignored (Sanders 1976, 165). Since only Marxist approaches are recognized in the United States as sociological (and rejected instantly for ideological reasons), Sammons comes to the pessimistic conclusion that the diverging literary methods are "a symptom for a much greater alienation between the two countries" than is generally assumed (Sammons 1978, 115) and that both countries would be better served if Germans and Americans did not know too much about each other. For example, Sammons writes, if Americans knew of the usually negative reaction of Germans to the popular slogan "Live free or die," the Americans would react with hostility. Freedom, Sammons concludes, is not as much a priority in Germany (or in other Western European countries) as in the United States.

Manfred Durzak, however, finds the American reading public genuinely interested in German literature, but he asserts, that the publishing industry does not provide continued access to the German book market. A general lack of German literature in America has often been recognized by critics who have felt that new English, French, and Italian fiction has been much more conspicuous in American bookstores than literature "from the land along the Rhine" (Burger 1957). Since this sporadic access to German literature does not provide enough continuous information about the situation in Germany for critics and readers, both groups show a sense of frustration about their ignorance. Ziltener notes that Americans feel they ought to know more about recent German history, but nobody is really serious about providing more information. Michael Wood speculates about possible reasons for this lack of interest when he senses among his fellow citizens a resentment against "the faint weirdness of daily life in a conformist country" (Ziltener 1982, 19). This clearly contradicts the presumed intellectual curiosity of the critics, and it seems to reflect the current situation in American-German relations: a courteous curiosity on the surface coupled with a more deeply rooted reservation about the former enemy. According to Wood, Germany, a country where "everything so aspires to order that the very slightest deviation smacks of a disturbing anarchy" (Wood 1975), is indeed not attractive to the average American reader. Since German history is so loaded, many critics partial to German society feel they could help the reception of German books more if they as critics did not refer to German social conditions, both historical and contemporary, but concentrated more on aspects of style and form.

2. The reception of Böll's works in the United States reflects that of German literature in general. According to Ray Lewis White (White 1979, 4), no post–World War II German author had become widely known in the United States in academic discussions or the general reading public until 1954. Böll provided in *And Never Said a Word* (1954)[1] the right subject matter and the right literary treatment to appeal to American readers, since it gave the American public a first glimpse of the miserable living conditions in Germany. It could be argued that Böll's novel *And Never Said a Word* was probably regarded more as a report than fiction and thus was not taken seriously by the more sophisticated literature critics, but its moderate success was an important asset in Böll's first reception. Richard Plant praised the book as "the beginning of a literary renaissance in Western Germany" (Plant 1954) and Böll as a born writer who "manages to distill . . . from the tristesse of its people a particular sweetness" in this novel. Similarly, Plant praised Böll's *Adam, Where Art Thou?*[2] as succeeding in "conjuring the agonies of W.W.II." Like many American critics who are familiar with only a few German titles, Plant compared Böll's book to Remarque's *All Quiet on the Western Front* but discovered weaknesses in Böll's book in comparison with Remarque's (Plant 1955). Such superficial comparisons are mostly due to the limited

---

[1] Translated again in 1978 by Leila Vennewitz as *And Never Said a Word* (New York: McGraw-Hill, 1978).

[2] Translated again by Leila Vennewitz in 1970 as *Adam and The Train: Two Novels* (New York: McGraw-Hill, 1970).

knowledge of German literature by most American critics.[1] With this book, American critics began using the word *compassionate* as a label for Böll's fiction. Unfortunately, this term turned out to be rather ambiguous, since it could be used pejoratively, indicating a lack of prose experimentation and an abundance of sentimentality (White 1979, 4). Similarly, the American-German émigré writer and critic Frederic Morton criticized Böll's *The Train Was on Time* as unconvincing to the average American reader unfamiliar with the details concerning the war on the eastern front (Morton 1956). These reviews give a representative impression of the first reactions to Böll's books in America: they were considered pale imitations of the German literature of the 1920s such as Remarque's acclaimed book or Fallada's novel *Little Man – What Now?*, the most recent works of German literature that educated Americans knew.

Billiards at Half-Past Nine (1961), like *And Never Said a Word*, was well received in the United States and "will likely remain Böll's best-known work in America" (White 1979, 6). The book's success convinced American critics that Böll could contribute "significant fiction." White's praise is reflected in the *Christian Science Monitor*'s review, where the book is described as "a work in the best tradition of the German novel, taking up the thread broken by the Third Reich, the thread spun by Remarque's *All Quiet on the Western Front* and Fallada's *Little Man – What Now?*" (20 July 1962). Although the moderately experimental style pleased those critics interested in formal experimentation, it was not appreciated by all critics, — for example, Siegfried Mandel, who described Böll's style as "old-fashioned" and as "putting narrative ahead of experimentation" (Mandel 1962, 8). Böll's modernism appeared to Mandel too repetitive in theme and symbolism. The most common praise for Böll's newly displayed, moderately difficult narrative technique was that he still had more interest in story than in style. This note of gratitude for the comprehensibility of *Billiards at Half-Past Nine* came from the more conservative critics and was to become central to Böll's reputation in the United States.

---

[1] Francis Keene (*NYT*, 20 October 1957), in his review compares Böll's writing to that of Hans Fallada and Erich Maria Remarque, who were both popular in the United States at that time.

With the advent of Günter Grass, the new literary star from Germany, America's critics all but withdrew their admiration from the cumbersome Böll. With only one novel, *The Tin Drum* (1959), Grass had already eclipsed Heinrich Böll's five novels. From the beginning, Americans liked Grass's intellectual satire and innovative prose experiments far better than Böll's pedestrian stories. Thus Böll was regarded as Germany's "literary spokesman" only from 1954 to 1959, when this honor was transferred to Grass. Doris Auerbach states that "the German writer who had the greatest influence on the attitude of the *New York Times Book Review* not only toward German literature but the German people as well, was Günter Grass," not Heinrich Böll (Auerbach, in Ziltener 1982, 6). According to the critic Donald Robinson, "Günter Grass has been the most actively political writer in Germany since Walter von der Vogelweide"; Böll is no longer mentioned in this record of top writers (Ziltener 1982, 85) – nor among newspaper reviews.

Both authors were later honored with the Nobel Prize for Literature by the National Academy of Sweden as authors of "comprehensible" fiction. Bruce Cook believes the award has never been conferred on talented writers, but "for moral, rather than strictly literary reasons – as though it were a kind of spiritual beauty contest to be won on the basis of the high-minded sentiments expressed in the work of this novelist or that poet" (Cook 1975, 17). That may indeed explain why novelists like Günter Grass do not win as many literary prizes as Heinrich Böll did; the Nobel Committee has the purpose of honoring writers for their "moral" and comprehensible fiction. While Grass is regarded as a technically brilliant writer, Böll is seen as embodying more typical German qualities.[1]

The withdrawal of American public favor from Böll was exacerbated by the publication of *The Clown* (1965), a book Americans generally did not like. Russian reviewers had rejected the book due to its complete lack of ideological direction, while American reviewers rejected the book because Böll seemed no longer interested in prose experiments. Americans generally felt that by establishing himself as a

---

[1] Even in the United States, it was not Günter Grass but Heinrich Böll who was eventually elected honorary member of the American Academy for Arts and Letters in 1974, a fact that confirmed Böll's popularity among academics in the United States.

writer more concerned with Weltanschauung than with narrative structure, Böll was moving away from Western traditions. The book displeased those American critics like Thomas Lask who were used to the "dispassionate, innovative and intellectualized fiction of Nabokov and Jon Barth"; Lask put away *The Clown* with a feeling that "an act of demolition is not necessarily a novel" (Lask, 1965). Other critics looked at Böll's book as "a kind of syrup" (Enright, 1965). It was not until 1975 that American academic scholarship would find a few kind words for *The Clown*, when Böll's novel was regarded more as a continuation of *Billiards at Half-Past Nine*, as a copy of the French *nouveau roman*. It was C. A. M. Noble who considered Böll's protagonist Schnier not as an individual person with a personal fate in the realistic tradition but rather as a "type" in Kafka's tradition, and he therefore considered the book almost a classic (Noble 1975, 157). Stephen Koch pointed out a similarity between Böll's *The Clown* and Saul Bellow's *Herzog*, both of which came to the American market in 1965; like Bellow, Böll emphasized story and message over form and style (Koch 1965). Böll was attractive to some reviewers, however, since in *The Clown* he engaged in the discussion of religious topics (Stewart 1974, 5-10).

Except for the two novels *And Never Said a Word* and *Billiards at Half-Past Nine*, only Böll's short stories impressed reviewers with their "old-fashioned, well-understood technique" (White 1979, 9). With these stories Böll had found his audience in those Americans who like a moralistic, compassionate, poignant story in the tradition of Hemingway (Bauke 1966). Sigrid Bauschinger said in her article that the experience of the Vietnam War contributed to the renewed popularity of Böll's wartime short stories (Bauschinger 1971).[1] *Absent Without Leave* and *End of a Mission* received some modest praise in the United States, although they were generally not popular in Germany. Eric Wensberg compared *Absent Without Leave* to Heinrich von Kleist's novella *Michael Kohlhaas* (1965), and Kurt Vonnegut saw the book as a large puzzle: "The reader must bring to each story his own understanding of Germans and the war, for the principal materials used by Heinrich Böll are blanks and holes" (Vonnegut 1965). And an English

---

[1] Published as *18 Stories*, translated by LeilaVennewitz (New York: McGraw-Hill, 1966).

reviewer called Böll's short novel *End of a Mission* "to date Böll's most delicately humorous book" (Thomas 1968). All of these reviews confirm that Böll had become a moderately well-known German author by 1970, although he was considered not nearly so popular or technically advanced as Günter Grass.

The reason for this modest popularity was primarily Böll's "realistic," "old-fashioned sentimentalism" that some reviewers still appreciated, because it reminded them of a "pre-Brechtian" world (Bauschinger 1971). In somewhat abrasive Marxist jargon, Rainer Nägele concluded that "typical American criticism relies almost exclusively on traditional bourgeois aesthetics of identification, which fails when confronted with a socially committed work just as it fails with the progressive bourgeois avant-garde" (Nägele "Aspects," 1976, 67). Nägele finds that several of the social problems Böll deals with in his literature had their parallels in the United States. However, since foreign texts about these problems are rarely discussed in social terms, "precisely those social problems which are most comparable to American problems encounter the strongest mechanisms of repression" (Nägele, "Aspects" 1976, 28).

Manfred Durzak, who was more interested in formal aspects than Nägele, interpreted Böll's lukewarm reception in the English-speaking countries as a sign of greater literary sophistication among readers there (Durzak 1971, 7). Similarly, Bernd Balzer shows how the American literary tradition can also be an advantage for Böll's work; since West German criticism relies on social criticism and compares the text with the represented reality, Americans, with their more aesthetically oriented interests and greater distance to society, can often provide new angles for the study of Böll's books (Balzer 1981, 37).

3. Academic writing about Böll in the Western Hemisphere resembles the pattern of reception in the Marxist countries: much as the academic reception of Böll's work in the Soviet Union had started earlier than in the German Democratic Republic, so the Americans were the first Western scholars to write extensively about Böll. The simple reason is that scholarship on living authors is more acceptable in the United States than in West Germany. Since dissertations are the academic work of young emerging literature professors, they were

looking for authors they could use in their foreign literature classes, where students prefer authors whose language they can understand. Therefore, the large group of Germanists, not the established book reviewers, became Böll's biggest lobbying group in the United States, although Böll's academic popularity would not have been possible without the earlier press reviews. Among academics the popularity "race" between Böll and Grass is much closer than in the general reading public; in the academic world Böll's works are received with as much enthusiasm as Grass's (Schaller 1988, 105). Among university professors, *Billiards at Half-Past Nine* is Böll's most popular book, whereas students prefer his *Lost Honor of Katharina Blum*. Unlike reviews for the general public, however, academic articles about Böll offer more detailed information about contemporary Germany, although the average academic reader would tend to be familiar with these social discussions (Ziltener 1982, 41).

Although it would be inaccurate to speak of hostility toward the United States, there was definitely a certain reserve in Böll's feeling toward this country. During his frequent trips to the United States, Böll maintained his distance from both academic and popular critics. Böll had certain feelings of resentment against the Americans stemming from the time immediately following World War II, when he had been taken prisoner by American troops in 1945. The constant harassment by American soldiers made him more aware and appreciative of his German identity (Rademann 1988, 13). And Böll, like most liberal and left-wing Germans during the 1960s, became critical of the American involvement in Vietnam. He despised American popular culture and mentioned particularly the TV series "Dallas" as poison for the mind. On the other hand, Böll was a strong admirer of American noncommercial literature and is well known as the translator of J. B. Salinger's *The Catcher in the Rye* into German. As a keen reader, Böll stated he knew American culture mainly through its literature, which to him constituted the best access into any culture. Despite some areas of misunderstanding between the Americans and Böll, there are many connecting points helpful to German and American scholars working to establish Böll's literary reputation in the United States.

One of the first Americans interested in Böll was Theodore Ziolkowski, who wrote about the Christian message in Böll's early work. By comparing Böll's beliefs with Albert Camus's existentialism, he came to the conclusion that although Böll accepts the Christian faith and Camus rejects it, both come as close to each other in their criticism of practical Christianity as is possible for an atheist and a devout Catholic (Ziolkowski 1962, 290). Ziolkowski concludes that "Böll and Camus agree in essence" and react similarly to similar social conditions. By concentrating on formal aspects of *Billiards at Half-Past Nine*, Ziolkowski works out a connection to Böll's Christian existentialism. Using a traditional interpretation method (New Criticism), Ziolkowski proposes that Böll's "book is like a fugue in which the fragmentation of existence is juxtaposed in counterpoint to the implicit ideal of solidarity" (Ziolkowski 1962, 286). Ziolkowski's essay is a good example for early Böll criticism, finding that content and formal aspects complement each other well. It is no coincidence that Ziolkowski's interest was aroused by a formally complex book like *Billiards at Half-Past Nine*, which he related in a detailed analysis to the complexities of Germany's social structure. In a second essay, Ziolkowski tried to show the continuity from *Billiards at Half-Past Nine* to *The Clown* in a presumed "madhouse perspective," which Ziolkowski compared to Dostoyevsky's approach in his novels. Although this comparison is essentially correct, as discussed above in the chapter on "Böll in the Soviet Union," Ziolkowski carries the comparison too far when he claims that Schnier, the Clown, is "the pharmacist of a madhouse who hands candied bombs to society" (Reich-Ranicki 1968, 266). This assessment holds true for *End of a Mission*, which Böll wrote with the idea of breaking art out of the perceived "padded cell" and in which he meant to use literature as a "time bomb." Ziolkowski, however, overstates Böll's intention of challenging society through his work by continuing the method used in *Billiards at Half-Past Nine*. By using a text-based method in an innovative way Ziolkowski was able to come quite close to Böll's intentions.

Elisabeth Trahan and Eva Schiefer's essay "The Imagery of Heinrich Böll's 'Betrachtungen über den irischen Regen'" shows the pitfalls of a text-based method reminiscent of the traditional British method of textual "close reading": their structural interpretation of a chapter of the *Irish Journal* fails to show any significant meaning behind the textual interpretation, although the authors intended to demonstrate how the text is related to "the moral problems created by the Second World War" (Trahan/Schiefer 1962, 299).

The first book-length study of Heinrich Böll's work in the West, by the German-Canadian scholar Wilhelm Johannes Schwarz (1968), echoes most of the earlier assessments and reservations of the popular Böll reception. Like the early newspaper reviews, Schwarz's book is an impressionistic review of Böll's work and fails to support most of his assertions with evidence. Since there was not enough criticism on Böll's work available at the time Schwarz wrote his book, he depended almost entirely on his intuition as a critic. Although revealing more of Schwarz's bias than scholarly works should, the book remains an important document for the reception of Böll. Schwarz is candid about his likes and dislikes. He prefers the early Böll, the short-story writer, and admits a complete lack of understanding of the later Böll, the novelist. What Schwarz appreciates in the early Böll is the moral orientation, his Christian, antinationalist and anti-militaristic orientation. Schwarz's condemnation of Böll's later epic work is strong when he accuses Böll of incompetence, stating Böll never quite masters the task he set out to accomplish, epic breadth. Since he feels Böll's style is too episodic and lacks consistency, to him both Böll's style and story line seem "pedestrian" (*hausbacken*; Schwarz 1968, 13). Schwarz ridicules Böll's intentions to promote through literature social change as a "domesticated revolution along the lines of the constitution" (*eine gezähmte Revolution im Rahmen des BGB*, Schwarz 1968, 13). Schwarz's criticism culminates in the opinion that Böll's work is currently widely overestimated in Germany and the United States by reviewers and readers alike; he thus demonstrates a political twist in his argument that discredits his entire "new critical" approach. Later anti-Böll criticism would always resort to cold-war propaganda, as demonstrated in Schelsky's famous attacks on Böll's work. And like Schelsky, Schwarz admits to a bias in his literary taste, preferring writers such as Günter Grass, Uwe Johnson, or Martin Walser to Böll (Schwarz 1968, 51).

After having established his personal aesthetic preferences, Schwarz undertakes a cursory analysis of Böll's novels and longer narratives prior to the publication of *Billiards at Half-Past Nine* in 1959, none of which is found acceptable except the *Irish Journal*. Schwarz praises this impressionistic travel book about Ireland as one of Böll's greatest achievements. According to Schwarz, the *Irish Journal* shows an "elegance in expression" which deviates sharply from the "poetic aberrations" of *The Bread of Those Early Years* (Schwarz 1968, 14). *Billiards at Half-Past Nine* passes Schwarz's judgment as well, due to Böll's deliberate use of advanced technique. *The Unguarded House*,[1] according to Schwarz, is an unfinished book containing "certain phrases and ideas which often do not fit with the course of action"; the entire book should have been shortened by at least one third (Schwarz 1968, 32).[2] The excessive length and the tediousness of Böll's novel stems from his technique of adding more "people, more action, more monologues to an otherwise already finished plot" (Schwarz 1968, 28). The result in most of his novels is a bloated story with redundant thoughts and characters. Similarly, Schwarz considers *The Clown* a tirade against Catholicism with a plot that seems completely unmotivated and artificial. The worst book, according to Schwarz, is Böll's *End of a Mission*, which he considers a stilted report and an attempt to mutilate the German language completely. According to Schwarz, Böll's poetic imagination ended with this book; he was now capitalizing on his fame, and "from now on he will criticize and nothing but criticize, with a raised finger and a sour face" (40).

Conservative American or Canadian reviewers such as Schwarz could not forgive Böll for getting increasingly interested in writing literature about moral issues, a change they considered treason of the high standards of pure literature. Since they measured all work against an imagined standard of pure literature, they moved further and further away from Böll's as his novels became more morally and politically involved. It is therefore not surprising that *Group Portrait with Lady* did not meet with much praise either; Schwarz describes it as "an average and above all, a very boring book" (*ein mittelmäßiges und vor allem ... ein sehr langweiliges Buch*; 50). Again, Schwarz criticizes Böll's use of language, "lasciviously messed-up prose" ("schlüpfrig

---

[1] Translated for the British edition by Mervyn Savill (London: Arco, 1957). The American edition has the title *Tomorrow and Yesterday* and was also translated by Mervyn Savill (New York: Criterion Books, 1957).

[2] "In diesem Werk erkennt man überdeutlich Bölls Technik, mit der er einen längeren Roman konzipiert: in ein fertiges Gerüst baut er Personen, Handlungen Monologe sowie bestimmte Phrasen und Gedankengänge ein, die er immer wieder einflicht, obwohl sie oft nicht recht in die jeweilige Entwicklung passen."

verkorkste Prosa"; 49), which he finds is no match to Günter Grass's strong and vulgar eroticism. By going back to the book he disliked the most, *End of a Mission*, Schwarz accuses Böll's literature of demonstrating a complete lack of poetic language, since Böll, as an engagé writer, is not interested in experiments with aesthetic form at all. Böll, in other words, is not a writer whom he, Schwarz, could recommend for study.

In the second part of his book, Schwarz gives an analysis of Böll's major characters, and here he touches upon some fields that were expanded later by other scholars. Schwarz first concentrates on Böll's women, who he concludes are mostly minor figures and are important only in their relationships to their male partners. The woman, however, is the preserver of faith and tradition in the man's life; she is the man's guide and helper in difficult times. Other critics would later expose Böll's myth of the saintly woman. A second of Schwarz's theses is also worthwhile, his comparative chapter on the "little man" character, whom Schwarz compares to a picaro figure, found in early German and Spanish novels. As with the female character, Schwarz's analysis of the weak male character was later modified by other reviewers exposing the class base of Böll's petit bourgeois characters.

4. The reception of Böll's literature in the United States changed in the 1970s when more and more readers realized the purpose and seriousness of Böll's political engagement. The German-American scholar Peter Demetz of Yale University, in his essay introducing Böll to the general reading public, outlines the predominant American perception of Böll's merits. While he describes *The Unguarded House* as a novel in the unpopular social-critical tradition, *Billiards at Half-Past Nine* is praised as one of the more important newer German novels because of its aesthetic achievements (Demetz 1970, 222).

Walter Sokel finds that in *Billiards at Half-Past Nine* the author achieves a necessary symbolic destruction of pride in Germany, both personal and national, in the final scene: "His (Walter Fähmel's) last act in the novel is to repeat symbolically the execution of his pride which his son has performed actually; he cuts into the birthday cake which had been presented to him in the shape of his famous abbey and joyfully proceeds to demolish it" (Sokel 1967, 28). Sokel also sees older German literary traditions in Böll's novels, for example Heinrich von Kleist's Romantic ideas in Böll's *The Clown*, Kleist's ideal of the marionette figure, "an ultimately Romantic and Rousseauistic ideal" (Sokel 1967, 34). Michael Perraudin would later pick up on this connection when he wrote about *The Clown* that a *Marionettentheater*-based pattern was planned for the work (Perraudin 1988, 120). He also maintained that Böll used patterns of Kleist's comedy *The Broken Jug* (*Der zerbrochene Krug*) for *End of a Mission* (Perraudin 1988, 123). However, the negative comments in America about *The Clown* and *End of a Mission* still outweighed the occasional positive ones. And so Frank Trommler saw in *The Clown* a change in post–World War II German literature, characterized by blunt political reasoning instead of formal artistic expression. Trommler objected to the use of narrative mode in *The Clown*; although he did not mistake Schnier's views for Böll's personal ones, he still lamented the use of a direct form of addressing sociopolitical problems in this novel (Trommler 1971, 107). The political engagement should have been part of the embedded narrative structure, according to Trommler, instead of a bluntly independent element; to him there is little difference between this narrative and a political pamphlet.

While the preceding articles focused on problems with style and technique in Böll's novels between 1954 to 1968, another group of critics in the United States concentrated on religious symbolism. By returning to Böll's earlier short stories and novels, these conservative critics wanted to establish a counterbalance to the social theories that emerged in West Germany around Böll's subversive Christian ideas. Wilhelm Grothmann elevates Böll's *And Never Said a Word* to an unpolitical existential sphere where Fred accepts anxiety and suffering as part of daily life (Grothmann 1971, 206). According to Grothmann, Böll wants to institute a religious system with his literature, a belief that is medieval in the certainty it provides its followers (Grothmann 1971, 202). Wolfgang Grothe emphasizes the conservative tendencies intended by this approach. Grothe also uses Böll's *And Never Said a Word* as his model when he rebuffs "progressively republican or democratic ..., socialist, liberal, or church-initiated revolutionary attempts" as inadequate for changing man's relationship to man: man needs to be "fundamentally renewed, i. e., re-Christened, remissioned in the sense of the agape" (Grothe 1973, 321).[1] These statements sound particularly out of touch with the Marxist student revolts then occurring in Germany and are obviously a direct confrontation with theorists who use Böll's work for their own progressive agenda.

It was again Theodore Ziolkowski who gave the American preoccupation with religious questions an exciting twist, when he combined the search for religious meaning with an analysis of narrative structure and symbolism. His essay "Typologie und 'Einfache Form' in *Gruppenbild mit Dame*" (Ziolkowski 1975, 123-40) has become a model for analysis of symbols. Ziolkowski compares Leni to a "secularized Christian saint"; she goes through a process of secularization as her humanity is elevated to "beatification" (*Seligkeit*), and the author's "report" is subsequently elevated through that process. Thus the fictitious author is the compassionate observer of the beatification process by keeping the minutes as postulator or *advocatus Dei*. Ziolkowski based his essay on an earlier comparative analysis in which he compared the various methods of turning religious topics into secular texts, for instance, in Joyce's *Ulysses* and Thomas Mann's *Doktor Faustus*, using Andre Jolles's classic method of reducing narratives to simple forms ("einfache Formen"; Ziolkowski 1972). A second source of this essay is in Ziolkowski's book review of *Group Portrait with Lady*, in which he described Leni's character as being the "spiritual center, holding together all the other characters by the force of her essential humanity" (Ziolkowski 1973, 17-24). His concept of structuring Leni's character around a religious concept gives his entire approach more focus. A more complex interpretation of Leni's religious dimension came from Ralph Ley, who claimed that Leni exists on two levels, as a religious symbol and as a real person, thus opening up interpretations of Leni's social dimensions (Ley 1973, 28).

---

[1] "Eine progressive republikanische oder demokratische Verfassung, sozialistische, liberalistische oder kirchlich institutionalisierte Erneuerungsversuche allein werden nie ausreichen, wenn nicht die ursprünglichen Beziehungen von Mensch zu Mensch in der Nachbarschaft, in der Ehe, in der Familie, in dem weiteren Umkreis der Verwandtschaft, das heißt, in den kleineren, überschaubaren Lebensbereichen, die Böll den Vorwurf des 'Provinzialismus' eingetragen haben, von Grund auf erneuert, und das heißt für den Dichter: rechristianisiert, remissioniert, im Sinne der Agape restituiert würden."

However, Ley's analysis is sketchy and therefore less useful than Ziolkowski's.

Ziolkowski's Princeton colleague Victor Lange explored the nineteenth-century origins of Böll's "realistic" narrative. German realism, Lange claims, is an idealistic realism, which developed a literary style in trying to find acceptable philosophical solutions in the face of idealistic hypotheses; Theodor Storm, Gottfried Keller, and Wilhelm Raabe are prime examples of this idealistic realism (Lange 1975, 100). Since Böll followed this nineteenth-century German tradition and not the British or French line, it is paramount for readers in English-speaking countries to understand the philosophical premises underlying Böll's seemingly realistic narratives to avoid reading them as realistic (in the sense of naturalistic) literature (Lange 1975, 108). Lange's essay helps the reader avoid particularly grave misreadings of Böll's fiction, such as Wilhelm Schwarz's confusion of author's intent with his protagonist's in The *Clown*. Analyzing literature from the author's ideological angle, known as *Ideologiekritik*, has since become common practice in Germany. It is not as widely practiced in America and may partially explain why American critics are often at a loss when confronted with an author with a realistic surface of writing that masks a political program.

Like West German critics in the 1950s, American critics were interested in Böll's earlier texts, especially the short stories. However, although the prevalent early West German criticism of short stories came from a conservative existentialist approach, American interpreters used their own essays as a corrective element to the politically daring analyses coming out of West Germany after the student revolts of the 1960s. Cesare Cases's Marxist interpretation of Böll's short story "Die Waage der Baleks" ("The Balek Scales") especially hit a raw nerve for some American interpreters, driving them to their desks to refute Cases's social criticism of the story. Where West German interpreters had emphasized the "fateful developments that change the life" of the people, not the miserable living conditions, as had been Böll's intention (Vogt 1972, 38), the American critic John Fetzer (like Cases) sees a "nagging persistence of the gray areas of doubt" about the story's ideological consistency that confuses the reader's perception of right and wrong. However, unlike Cases, Fetzer praised Böll's fuzziness as literary ingenuity, since it turns the short story into more than a mere propaganda piece (Fetzer 1967, 473). What Cases regarded as a major weakness in Böll's ideological thinking was rated positively by Fetzer, who is highly suspicious of any logical reference system for a poet. It remains unclear what Fetzer regarded as the purpose of this story, compared with Cases's interest in ideological enlightenment. He only knew that this story reinforces the notion that "the clamor for reform in the present" is "equivocated by the clichés from the past," in other words, according to his interpretation political action is doubtful.

"Doctor Murke's Collected Silences" became one of the most discussed stories among American scholars. Erhard Friedrichsmeyer analyzes the story as a model satire and wants to illuminate "the satirical structures and techniques and thereby confirm Böll's reputation as satirist" (Friedrichsmeyer 1981, 4). Friedrichsmeyer believes strongly in relating German to American scholarship; his approach shows an application of Northrop Frye's theory of satire to Böll's short stories. In his praise for Böll as satirist, Friedrichsmeyer puts Böll in the tradition of Swift (and Voltaire). At the bottom of Friedrichsmeyer's investigation is his belief that we should not separate different literary genres, but make "generic differences based on modes of sensation" ("generische Unterscheidungen, die auf Empfindungsweisen beruhen"; Friedrichsmeyer 1981, 20). Friedrichsmeyer separates different representations of sensations as "modes," and, by using Frye's categories, he works out paradigmatic lines, various patterns of confrontation, of myths, of "the satirical signature," and other structural patterns of opposites in Böll's stories. In his "patterns of confrontation" Friedrichsmeyer finds textual opposites in Böll's prose – in "Doctor Murke's Collected Silences," Böll uses two opposite sets of terms: those of cutting and pasting and those of talking and being silent ("Schneiden und Kleben," "Reden und Schweigen"; Friedrichsmeyer 1981, 35). This seems to be the first application of any structural analysis of this type to Böll's texts. At the time of its publication it found little resonance in Germany although Friedrichsmeyer's American colleagues praised his book, — for example, Helmut Müssener, who applauded the book for countering the common opinion that "Böll is mainly an author more interested in content instead of problems of composition" (Müssener 1985, 377).[1]

Some American reviewers were skeptical of such an approach, for example Henry Glade, who prefers Robert Conard's "succinct and incisive interpretation" to Friedrichsmeyer's "diffuse" approach (Glade 1984, 503). The merit of Friedrichsmeyer's approach lies in its strict application of literary categories, by which he can show Böll's competence as a first-class writer. Friedrichsmeyer later expanded his concept on Böll as a satirist, and claims that Böll's work proves his own supposition that "one cannot be Christian and satirist alike. You have to choose and be the one or the other" (Friedrichsmeyer 1985, 206). As an author Böll later became politically and emotionally too involved to display the distance necessary for a good satirist.

Friedrichsmeyer was also interested in the picaresque as a mode. He argues that Böll's protagonists are both utopian and picaresque heroes, a theory Wilhelm Schwarz had introduced in his book – the existential failure of Böll's heroes is predetermined by their antagonistic elements. In *The Clown*, for example, we do not find the typical adventure structure of a picaresque novel with a curve going up and down; Schnier's line goes straight down (Friedrichsmeyer 1986, 161). And in *End of a Mission*, the Gruhls' anarchism shows a responsibility for the world that the traditional "foolish" picaro lacks. With this, Friedrichsmeyer argues, Böll expands the picaresque concept from its traditional form to a more modern one (Friedrichsmeyer 1986, 172).

In an essay for Böll's 75th anniversary, Friedrichsmeyer explores the "sentimental" as a mode that expresses his compassion and his responsibilities to his fellow citizens, as "a sign of a firm heart" (als "Ausdruck humaner Wachsamkeit, verantwortlicher Mitmenschlichkeit: 'Zeichen eines festen Herzens'"; Hoffmann 1992, 22). Friedrichsmeyer argues against the common German notion that the sentimental is unsuitable for expression in literature, and by again using Anglo-American traditions, he claims the sentimental is a part of the American democratic tradition where the aesthetic value is a value among others, and "its origin is the same [democratic] heart with which the democrat gains his moral identity" (Friedrichsmeyer 1992, 183).[1] Friedrichsmeyer recognizes a difference between the early

[1] ". . . Böll sei ein vornehmlich thematisch ausgerichteter Autor, der an kompositorischen Fragen desinteressiert sei."

[1] ". . . Sein Ursprung ist dasselbe Herz, mittels dessen der Demokrat seine moralische Identität gewinnt."

Böll, where the sentimental exceeds the limits of aesthetic taste and the later Böll, especially in *Women in River Landscape*. In Böll's last novel, Friedrichsmeyer descibes Böll's application of the sentimental in combination with the absence of an author as a typical postmodern style of writing (Friedrichsmeyer 1992, 193) – a label that most Anglo-Saxon reviewers seem to agree with (e.g., Reid 1988). Friedrichsmeyer also perceives a decline in Böll's ability to write succinct short stories. By the 1970s Böll's stories have lost their "denseness" and have become "discursive" (Friedrichsmeyer, "Short Stories" 1985, 63). Friedrichsmeyer regrets that Böll has now become more concerned with "the authenticity, the social energy, and the constructiveness of personal relationships," and less with formal aspects (65).

B: The German Model

1. Ten years after Marxist students and professors had all but banished linguistic methods and text-centered (*text-immanente*) interpretations from German literary scholarship, a similar change occurred in the United States. It began in 1982 with Robert Conard, who introduced a method integrating textual analysis with an investigation of German social conditions. Conard rejected Fetzer's interpretation of "The Balek Scales" and instead considered it one of Böll's important works. Conard saw this text as the first in which Böll examined and condemned the economic conditions of society – a theme seen throughout his entire work (Conard 1981, 62). Conservative critics can usually be separated from more progressive ones by their preference for the early Böll, and Conard was one of the first American critics to look to the later Böll as a model. This pattern developed in Germany as well as in America, except that conservatives were a marked majority in the United States. In an earlier essay, when Conard compared Böll's with Brecht's political viewpoint, he concluded that Brecht saw the world through the eyes of ideology, whereas Böll saw it with the eyes of compassion, an important distinction between the radical ideologue Brecht and the humanist Böll (Conard 1978, 101).

However, despite his distinction between Böll's approach and Brecht's, Conard used Marxist phraseology to interpret Böll's intentions. In working with "The Balek Scales," he described Böll's fictional

world as one totally controlled and manipulated by capitalist interests, as when the Baleks regulate both "the base and the super-
structure of society," as Conard phrases it. However, Conard shows
that despite Böll's skepticism about a totally controlled political
world, Böll follows principally Marxist thinking in believing "that
justice is impossible within this (capitalist) system" (Conard 1978,
108). Conard argues that Böll with this short story criticizes the
shortcomings of our own society as if it were dominated by a
primitive capitalism at the turn of the century. To Conard the text is a
clear Marxist parable and definitely achieves its educational purpose.
It also partially achieves Brecht's ideal of popularity (*Volkstümlichkeit*),
making a work of art understandable to the masses by writing from
their own point of view. According to Conard "The Balek Scales"
fulfills Brecht's demand for realism by emphasizing historical development and societal mechanism, eventually unmasking the
prevailing social viewpoint as that of the ruling class. Although
Conard argues that Böll's basic premises are Marxist, he is also eager
to point out non-Marxist or non-Brechtian elements in the story: by
focusing on the illegal injustice of the scales and not the legal injustice
of the Balek system, Böll does not engage in a critical analysis of the
political system (*Ideologiekritik*) but shows his nonideological view of
society. With this essay, Conard was the first to balance the conservative tendency in American Böll research, which had already begun to
dominate the American discussion, with its innerliterary criteria.

Subsequently Conard criticized Friedrichsmeyer's interpretation of
Böll's short story "Nicht nur zur Weihnachtszeit" by maintaining that
the "results are sometimes forced from the text" (Conard 1984, 97–
103). He criticized Friedrichsmeyer's emphasis on the critique of
Germany's return to a prewar middle-class comfort (*Bürgerlichkeit*) as
too narrow and instead pointed to a more general interpretation of the
story. By stressing Böll's attempt in this story to show how the
Germans failed to work out their problems with the past, Conard
claims the story can be understood by a larger audience. The story's
conditions, though specifically German, can also be applied to those in
the United States. Thus Conard is one of the first American interpreters who saw Böll's literature not only as isolated documents of
German social life but also as texts that should have an impact on
America. The story can, in fact, be read with the same interest in any

country where a shameful past has not been adequately dealt with. If applied properly, Conard's method would greatly enhance the popularity of Böll's fiction in this country.

Conard's book, published by Twayne, summarized very well the level that American Böll scholarship had achieved in the late 1970s, just as Wilhelm Schwarz had summarized the prevailing attitudes of the 1960s. Unlike Schwarz, Conard offers no off-the-cuff comments on Böll's works but summarizes "as a student of German" the existing theories and opinions on Böll; he does not attempt to offer a new approach. Since Americans had largely focused on Böll's short stories, Conard felt it necessary to reflect this interest in his book, of which approximately half is dedicated to Böll's early work. As in his essay, Conard praises "Doctor Murke's Collected Silences" and "The Balek Scales" as "Böll's most highly regarded work" (Conard 1981, 47). Except for Conard's high praise for these two stories, the content of the first part of his book does not differ markedly from Schwarz's earlier book. It should be noted that Conard offers some very good summaries of the recent critical writings by Ziolkowski and Durzak.

At the turning point between Böll's earlier and later works (between *Billiards at Half-Past Nine* and *The Clown*), Conard's book becomes more interesting. With his interest in socio-economic criticism, which could be described as a modified Frankfurt School approach, he shows a great appreciation for the later Böll. Conard criticizes *Billiards at Half-Past Nine* as a book that does not offer criticism of the economic nature of capitalism, "but of only its militaristic and political aspects" (135). It is obvious that Conard had expanded his method from his earlier review of "The Balek Scales" in which it had become apparent to him that Böll had begun to examine and condemn the economic conditions of society. Conard goes on to analyze each book from a similar "socio-structural" viewpoint. He comes to the conclusion, as did the East German critic Günter Wirth, that Böll's "Stifter's Epilogue" as a text challenges middle-class premises propagated in Stifter's nineteenth-century novel *Der Nachsommer* (90). And in *The Bread of Those Early Years*, Conard states, Böll does not simply depict love and the injustices of the economic system through the bread symbol; the entire novella is in fact "a parable of the economic system" (117). By looking at social conditions as catalysts for Böll's novels, Conard regards *The Clown* as Böll's answer to the increasingly conservative social climate in the Federal Republic in the late 1950s. *The Clown* reflects Böll's ambition in the early 1960s to develop "away from optimism toward negativism, away from chastising to pillorying West German society" (143). The failure of *End of a Mission,* according to Conard, is due to Böll's "decency," reflected in the harmonious way of life presented in the novel. Therefore Böll's ideal of a new humanity is "lost in the very decency of this Rhenish village life" (158). As for *Group Portrait with Lady,* Conard describes Leni's character as Mary (as did Ziolkowski), the character of her lover Boris as Joseph, and their son Lev as a Christ figure. However, Conard maintains his basic socio-economic approach for this book as well when he asserts that it is impossible "to be a Christian and support a society based on exploitation" (182). Since no significant research about *The Lost Honor of Katharina Blum* had been written in America by the time Conard's book was published, he does not have much to say other than calling the book the most political of all of Böll's works.

Despite his scant interpretations of Böll's last two novels, Conard's book became influential in helping develop a critical approach in American Böll scholarship by learning more from the German political methods rather than relying on American text-based approaches. Conard was the first to realize that in order to do justice to the political intentions of an author like Böll, a critic has to abandon his preconceived critical approach and instead tailor his method to the author. With Conard's book, readers in the United States began to appreciate the full scope of Böll's craftsmanship; in fact, later articles on *Group Portrait with Lady* and *The Lost Honor of Katharina Blum* would not have been possible without Conard's ground-breaking work.

2. With the publication of Böll's "political" novels *Group Portrait with Lady* (1973) and *The Lost Honor of Katharina Blum, or, How Violence Develops and Where It Can Lead* (1975), American critics began to see Böll's literature more along Conard's lines and to adjust their approach to do justice to Böll's intentions. This change in reception patterns coincided with the discovery of Böll as a serious author by American Germanists with a neo-Marxist inclination and marks the beginning of the Germanization of American Böll scholarship; it also

demonstrates the necessity of following political events in Germany closely in order to apply this method correctly.

In his 1976 book on Böll's reception, Rainer Nägele offered an approach that is somewhat influenced by his interpretation of Adorno's ideas in the Frankfurt School. In an essay of the same year,[1] Nägele condemned most American critics as "traditionally bourgeois" and maintained that critics in this country show a "complete neglect of social context" in treating works from different traditions with the same "human" approach in order to achieve a universally readable literary canon. Nägele pleaded for a change in the reception pattern (Nägele, "Aspects" 1976, 45-68). Like other orthodox GDR Marxists (especially Bernhard) before him, Nägele rejected Böll's vague utopian dreams as idyllic, although he viewed Böll's imagery as "convincing." Böll's major shortcoming, then, is his "precipitous resolution of contradictions," which never gets to the core of the matter (Nägele, "Aspects" 1976, 46). Nägele criticizes Böll for turning away from the real problems of the world by presenting a small, limited world peopled with certain types of figures, "primarily petty bourgeois characters, the victims of society, eccentric figures whose eccentricity constitutes an anarchic protest against society" (62). And, by characterizing Böll's protagonists as "petty bourgeois" who usually appear as innocent victims, Nägele condemns Böll's glorification of the petit bourgeoisie as "ignoring its real role in National Socialism," namely as Hitler's major support group. Böll's preference for victim figures reflects the social contrast between above and below in a simple aesthetic pattern. Since it is not historically true that the Nazis victimized the petit bourgeoisie, Nägele writes, Böll's texts cannot and should not be regarded as instructions for political analysis and action. Without examining all of Nägele's arguments, it can be said that his position is almost orthodox Marxist, and thus his praise for the East German Marxist Bernhard's study as an excellent "dialectical examination of form and content" should come as no surprise (65). Nägele criticizes the study by the other important East German critic, Wirth, as hardly Marxist in its strange combination of "an obviously conservative theology with socialist phraseology" (66). However, Nägele agrees with Wirth in praising Böll's style for its mass appeal,

[1] As mentioned in chapter II. A. in this book.

breaking through that "magic" boundary between serious and popular literature (57).

Despite his harsh criticism of Böll's political line as inadequate, Nägele claims that Böll did not exhibit the standard modernist failure to create a meaningful language, as for example Samuel Beckett does in his plays. Nägele claims that Böll, unlike "high modern" writers such as Beckett, did not totally reject language as senseless since the communicative discourse was occupied by strategies of power but instead used traditional discourse and expanded it in his "strategy of the minimal difference" (Nägele 1977, 202).[1] Here, then, would be a starting point for a reception analysis of Böll's literature studying to what extent Böll's proximity to certain forms of popular literature creates certain "horizons of expectation" according to Jauß's reception theory. The difference in the textual structure between established and innovative discourse, however small it may be, rather than the political action in the text itself, manifests Böll's political engagement. Nägele would argue that if one simply concentrates and analyzes the content of Böll's novels and short stories, the discussion would get into a political debate that Böll would obviously lose because of the political inconsistencies in his program; an aesthetically oriented interpretative technique, however, would do more justice to his original intentions, which are more literary than political.

By concentrating on aesthetic merits rather than political content, Nägele shows his training in the "American" textual tradition; however, he also advances certain Marxist positions being discussed in Germany at that time (Bernhard). Nägele's proposition of a reception-centered aesthetic of the minimal difference was not pursued in Böll research either in the United States or in Germany; in all probability it proved too abstract. Instead, different German Marxist approaches to Böll were taken up and centered around the periodical specializing in those approaches, *New German Critique*.

Donna Baker pursued Nägele's accusation of Böll's indiscriminate use of the *Kleinbürger* image in an article for *New German Critique* and charged that Böll shows in his novels disgusting petit bourgeois characters (Baker 1975). Her view, labeled Marxist, seems basically in-

---

[1] "Böll, so scheint es, versucht dem Dilemma dadurch zu entgehen, daß er scheinbar auf vertraute Diskursformen eingeht, sie dann aber in der Strategie der kleinen Differenz verschiebt und verunsichert."

tolerant in its condemnation of people who are too anchored in Germany and know little of other countries. She claims that more cosmopolitan writers such as Max Frisch with his novel *Homo Faber* appeal much more to American readers (Baker 1975, 102). But unlike Nägele, Baker comes to the conclusion that Böll presents an accurate picture of German society, since his books "reveal the background of the little folk who more or less support the overall social-political reality of 1933-1945: Nazism" (Baker 1975, 104). With her praise of Böll's realism, Baker accepts Lukács's view, as Nägele had, that Böll shows a harmonious nineteenth-century world, and she finds that the literary representation of middle classes in the nineteenth century produced certain modes of realistic description. Baker claims Böll showed modern mass society through an inadequate and anachronistic writing style; he wrote his war novels in a style not in harmony with "modern" modes of writing (105). Baker concludes that the aesthetic anachronism of Böll's writing results from the social backwardness of German society in general. This view, albeit not forcefully presented, might explain the reluctance of some American intellectuals to get involved with Germany; they perceive that society as more backward than their own.

3. Besides Robert Conard and Rainer Nägele, Jack Zipes, one of the editors of *New German Critique* who identifies with the West German leftist cause, was the only notable exception in this reluctance to get involved with Germany's social problems. He critically analyzes the West German situation in the arts of the period from 1972 to 1975 and subscribes to the West German neo-Marxists' viewpoint rejecting current society as one in which "an atmosphere of fear and hysteria has been created causing the average citizen practically to identify radicalism (i.e., socialism, Marxism) with terrorism" (Zipes 1977, 75). For an average citizen, it is impossible to gain correct information about the power structure in West German capitalist society because of the deliberate disinformation through the media (Zipes 1977, 85). According to Zipes, Katharina Blum is not at all atypical of the present-day West German citizen, who completely complies with the laws of the state and tends to be unquestioningly obedient. It is apparent that Böll wanted to present an idealistic model in Katharina. Zipes agrees with Nägele's assessment that Böll's understanding of

social causes was limited and that Böll was unable to portray the political repression in Germany in this book (80).[1] Subsequently Zipes concludes that both Böll's book as well as Schlöndorff's film[2] are unable to uncover the degree to which West Germans have already internalized their country's repressive power structure and have become "legislators of their own fear" (82). The country is dominated by the media that serve capitalist interests of disinformation. However, in comparing the film with the novella, Zipes concludes that Böll's novella is able to show how language is being used and should be used for understanding social and political relationships. When Schlöndorff rewrote the book for his film adaptation, he eliminated Böll's subtle differences in language and retained only melodramatic effects, which are a problem of the original novel, according to Zipes (84).

Of the few radical Marxists to carry the torch from West Germany to the United States, Zipes gives a thoroughly political assessment of the failure of both the book and the movie in claiming that their weaknesses as political works tell us more about West Germany's political reality than their actual messages: "The potential for art works to be politically efficacious, to take hold of problems and make them meaningful in our everyday lives depends upon the quality of the political action in a given period" (84). And in a true Lukácsian twist in his interpretation, Zipes regards Böll's failure as a reflection of the entire political system; much as the act of violence by Katharina Blum is an act of frustration, Böll's and Schlöndorff's artistic works result from a breakdown in the public discourse and in their bungled technique show "a frustrated struggle to break the stranglehold of repression that maims expression" (84).

Zipes's approach found some imitators in emerging American feminist scholarship. Charlotte W. Ghurye, for example, sees Katharina Blum as a symbol of women's social degradation and contends that her act of revenge is a solution to her denigration on a personal level only. She concludes from the book "that a woman can use a gun as efficiently as a man when it comes to defending her

---

[1] Zipes praises Peter Schneider's *Schon bist du ein Verfassungsfeind* as a book that clearly shows the existing power structures in the Federal Republic.

[2] Schlöndorff, Volker. 1975. *Die verlorene Ehre der Katharina Blum.*

honor" (Ghurye 1976, 75). This assessment seems a lot closer to the
social reality of the United States than that of West Germany! There
were several more attempts to introduce Marxist interpretative
techniques into Anglo-American readings of Böll, for example, H. E.
Beyersdorf's essay, in which he tries to uncover Herbert Marcuse's
refusal-principle in *Group Portrait With Lady* (Beyersdorf 1983), o r
Yvonne Holbeche's rejection of Durzak's and Vogt's assessment of
End of a Mission as an unpolitical idyll, stating "that art can pose a
threat to the political interests of the establishment" (Holbeche 1980,
413); however, none of these attempts reached the intellectual level of
Nägele and Zipes.

C: Misjudgment or Integration?

1. Voices like Nägele's and Zipes's remained isolated among
American critics, who analyzed primarily innerliterary phenomena in
Böll's texts. American critics did not react to *The Lost Honor of
Katharina Blum* with Nägele's social criticism but by returning to the
established formalistic modes of interpretation. The reviewer in the
New Yorker characterizes the institutional conflicts in *The Lost Honor of
Katharina Blum* as a manifestation of the psyche of the German people,
asserting that the people and the institutions in the story are uniquely
and unmistakably German and that it is Böll's understanding of these
German conditions that makes the book worthwhile (*New Yorker* 1975,
119). Representative of this method is the interpretation of *The Lost
Honor of Katharina Blum* in an introduction to West German literature
in which the novel is summarized as "the pure and innocent female
seduced by a man and destroyed by a relentless society" (Franklin
1979, 38). The character of Katharina is, according to this reading, "one
of the standard figures of Western literature" (Franklin 1979, 38).

Since the first collection of Böll's essays was published in 1977, just
two years after *The Lost Honor of Katharina Blum*, this concentrated
presentation of Böll's radical political views was overwhelming for his
American readers.[1] The *New York Times* reviewer complains about
Böll's Nobel lecture, which was reprinted in the collection of his

---

[1] *"Missing Persons "and Other Essays*, trans. Leila Vennewitz (New York: McGraw-
Hill, 1977).

essays, and quips that "even the legendary patience of the Swedish Academy may have been tried by Mr. Böll's Nobel lecture" (Broyard 1977). The reviewer accuses Böll of generalizing about writers and writing and therefore finds his essays much more boring to read than his short stories about World War II. Other critics agreed: "Most of these essays are far below the literary level of Böll's fiction" (Masterton 1977). One of the best examples of this reaction can be seen in Michael Wood's review for the *New York Times*, in which he compares Böll's writing with Kafka's, since according to Wood, "Kafka created a literary language that could contemplate enormities, and Böll, intentionally or not, avails himself of that language" (Wood 1975). In his interpretation Wood argues, following Adorno, that it has became impossible to write about poetry after Auschwitz, and claims that "Kafka's voice is one of the very few voices the Germans can still use" (Wood 1975). Germany is seen as a remote society with a grotesque history that does not resemble anything familiar to Americans. Although sympathetic to Böll's book, Wood's allusion to Kafka's grotesque world portrays Germany as departing so far from Western humanist traditions that it appears alien and completely unfamiliar. Thus Wood's review is a mixed blessing for German studies, as he overinterprets Böll's depiction of inhumanity in *The Lost Honor of Katharina Blum*. While an interested reader might accept the book as appealing in the context of Kafka, Wood's reading of Böll turns the reader even further away from an appreciation of modern Germany.

Mark W. Rectanus analyzed the reasons for the problematic reception of Böll's book in the United States, and he came to a similar pessimistic conclusion. Rectanus felt that Germany was to a large extent still perceived within the context of the United States' experience in World War II and that most American reviewers did not even bother to differentiate between the Federal Republic of Germany and the German Democratic Republic (Rectanus 1986, 265). None of the reviewers of *The Lost Honor of Katharina Blum* attempted to relate the book to an analysis of political, social, or economic institutions, or to the role of the media in the Federal Republic; instead, they focused on the love story between Ludwig and Katharina, according to Rectanus. However, James Reid reports that in England the school edition of *The Lost Honor of Katharina Blum*, published in 1980, has become one of the most popular German texts for sixth-graders, despite serious conservative criticism of the book in Great Britain (Reid 1988, 181). The British anti-Böll criticism was more straightforwardly political than the American, which definitely displayed a lack of interest in German political events. Britain is, after all, a lot closer to Germany, and most German matters have a more direct impact on British life.

The American lack of interest, however, is not limited to books about Germany – any book in a foreign literature published in English is usually isolated from its native culture and reviewed in a cultural vacuum. Further evidence for this intentional cultural isolation is Hollywood's remaking of foreign films, especially French ones. Producers argue that the films are adapted to American conditions since Americans are not expected to be familiar with living conditions in foreign countries. Since Hollywood was not interested in promoting Schlöndorff's movie version of *The Lost Honor of Katharina Blum*, Americans saw instead a TV adaptation entitled *The Lost Honor of Kathryn Beck*, which aired January 24, 1984, on CBS and starred Marlo Thomas as Kathryn Beck and Kris Kristofferson as her lover Ludwig Götten (Rectanus 1986, 262-63).

J. P. Stern's attack on Böll resembles the politically motivated criticism by Matthias Walden and Hans Habe in Germany.[1] However, Stern's assault, which appeared first in the London *Times* (Stern 1976) and was reprinted in Dell'Agli's book, has a certain Anglo-American touch to it when he compares Böll to Grass and specifies why he prefers the latter (Stern 1984). Like many conservative critics before him, Stern estimates Böll's artistic qualities below those of Grass, who, Stern maintains, has been able to illustrate the German political predicament much better and with more strength. However, Stern's main allegation concerns Böll's ideology, since his values appear to be clichéd. They are – and here Stern presents a unique new idea – "a mechanical reversion of the Nazi ideology" (Stern 1984, 104),[2] a deliberate connection of Böll's thinking with that of the Nazis. Stern maintains that Böll proclaims his belief in the strength of the individual

---

[1] Hans Habe and Matthias Walden were Böll's main conservative critics in West Germany. See particularly chapter III. C. in this book.

[2] "Sie gipfeln in einer rein mechanischen Umkehrung des nationalsozialistischen Wertschemas . . . ."

where the Nazis proclaimed the glory of the martial national group. And whereas the Nazis glorified the will and political power, Böll's characters are full of doubt; for them power is in itself evil. Stern sees Böll as leaving the traditions of the Enlightenment, the tradition of the most admirable German writers such as Thomas Mann and Erich Kästner. Although these writers did not have a political program themselves other than to follow a blind belief in the progressive nature of history, Stern admires their faith in the Enlightenment over Böll's nihilism. Stern comes to the conclusion that Böll's work is a total negation of the Nazi concept and that it seems as if his work were inspired primarily as a direct response to the Nazis. Stern concludes his pamphlet by asserting that Böll's attitude as an underdog does not help produce great literature. Stern misunderstands Böll's intentions as a writer who never wanted to write "great literature" in the first place; he was more interested in writing morally correct literature and, with his writings, helping Germans to understand themselves and their country's past. As Stern's article shows, his interest in form and language is only superficial and hides his primarily political arguments.[1]

2. It is important to separate politically motivated text analyses like Stern's attack from academic approaches. Since text-immanent interpretations were not considered "politically correct" in Germany during the 1970s they were done by Germanists not limited to one political outlook. The essays in this section demonstrate that it was still possible to come to interesting conclusions by applying text-based methods to the text. The British academic and literary critic Stephen Smith was one of the first to employ a strictly language-oriented method in the discussion of Böll's *The Lost Honor of Katharina Blum*. Not surprisingly, he comes to a negative impression of the book, condemning, for example, Böll's indiscriminate use of the word *nice* (*nett*), which, he says, produces a "carpet of niceness" (*Nettigkeitsteppich*, Smith 1975, 105).

William Sewell summarizes current interpretations of the novella's narrative structure: those which described the book as "overflowing in structure" ("Übermaß an Konstruktion"), with "playful flashbacks"

---

[1] See Karl Heinz Bohrer's reply to Stern (Bohrer 1976).

("spielerische . . . Rück- und Vorblenden"; Rolf Michaelis, in Sewell 1982, 182) and what originates in the narrator's scruples about finding the right words, allowing us as readers to share in his discoveries with a critical eye. Sewell focuses particularly on Manfred Durzak's structural comparison of *The Lost Honor of Katharina Blum* with *Group Portrait with Lady*, where, according to Sewell, Durzak omitted a thorough demonstration of the formal mechanisms by which the narrator/author organizes his material. Sewell attempts to investigate the mechanisms operating behind the author's strategies, the novella's major structural element (169). He sets about to correct Durzak's assumption that the book is a failure as a political pamphlet because it offers no realistic solution to a political problem with Katharina's essentially private protest on the "questionable practices" of the tabloids (176). Sewell wants to correct Durzak's contention that *Katharina Blum* fails as a work of art, because the author's strategy "is forced to capitulate" (176) in front of the task of bringing together the content and the formal construction.

Sewell contends that Durzak fails to do justice to both Böll's intentions and to his artistry, and asks instead whether realistic political solutions can be expected from a work of fiction. Sewell concludes that "the narrator seems to lose control of his material precisely because there can be no satisfactory outcome: while Katharina's individual protest may provide a temporary catharsis, it reduces even further her hard-earned social integrity and is politically futile" (Sewell 1982, 176). The "evidence of a paradoxical harmony in disharmony" that Sewell uncovered in his analysis is proof of a disquieting "systematic working of 'structural violence'" ("strukturelle Gewalt," 177). This analysis clearly develops the dynamic potential in Böll's novella.

Compared with this analysis relating the structure and content of *The Lost Honor of Katharina Blum*, other interpretations are inadequate. Margit Sinka, for example, discusses the text as a novella and, besides retelling the story at great length, focuses on the role of the narrator. Sinka, however, comes to the conclusion that it is still too early to tell whether from the perspective of an investigation into the history of the genre, Böll's narrator causes the work to stray into a generic category other than the novella (Sinka 1981, 171). She wonders whether the genre concept of the novella has been expanded through the narrator's strategies, introducing a new genre of "docu-fiction." Although it might be interesting for this critic to investigate novellas in a comparative manner, her analysis becomes too form-oriented in its approach to be truly useful.

In the 1980s many American and British critics concentrated on all of Böll's novels, indicating that Böll's work had now reached the mainstream of British-American research; Böll had become a classic. The main focus continued to be on formal aspects, such as Diane Stevenson's examination of the temporal aspect in America's favorite book by Böll, *Billiards at Half-Past Nine.* Like Durzak and Bernhard, Stevenson relates structure to meaning, but she expands Böll's system of symbolic opposites to make it a general structuring device for the way the world is perceived in this novel. Böll's buffaloes and lambs are related to the opposing forces of chaos and coherence, both of which make up his concept of morality (Stevenson 1990, 105). She concludes that the lesson of time is found in history, the novel's major structuring device is its flashbacks, and the lessons for the future are to be found in a new morality that overcomes history (Stevenson 1990, 113). Although not as convincing as Durzak's and Bernhard's essays, Stevenson's shows how Americans are now using more and more interpretative approaches relating structure to meaning.

Some reviewers hide their political agenda in a discussion of the narrative structure, as in the discussion of violence in Böll's novels. Linda Hill relates the structure of *The Lost Honor of Katharina Blum* to Böll's perceived political intention and writes that *The Lost Honor* is the first novel in which Böll takes violence against villains seriously. Hill claims that the violence in this novel is denounced by means of the "narrative structure" (Hill 1981, 155). However, the narrative structure or story line could, with its open-endedness, support either claim. Perhaps the perceived open-endedness is important for Hill for political reasons, as she wants to emphasize Böll's pacifism.

Mark Cory also attacks Böll for the use of violence in his novel *The Safety Net* and asserts that it was inserted only to spice up the seedy love story. Cory charges that terrorism and genuine physical violence are employed to a degree unparalleled in Böll's fiction. Böll uses the word *gesalzen* ("salted") for a pastry concealing a bomb, while, on the other hand, a letter having no explosive is described as dynamite and a child is labeled as highly explosive (Cory 1988-1989, 48). The line between reality and violence is deliberately unmarked in this novel, according to Cory; our normal sense of danger is defeated by Böll's use of words, whereas, one might add along Cory's line of thinking, it should have been Böll's duty to warn against the Baader-Meinhof Group and not against the terrorism of the state.

The British critic Herbert Waidson rejects this novel as well. He rejects Leni's actions as irrelevant by his comparing the two time levels in the presentation of events of World War II and their relationship to the present West German situation in the novel. Waidson comes to the conclusion that the crisis of Leni's eviction is a much less serious threat than the events surrounding her and Boris's withdrawal to the catacombs twenty-five years earlier and that events during the short history of the Federal Republic affect people's lives much less than "the much closer presence of immediate and irreparable disaster in 1944-45" (Waidson 1973, 130). Waidson's method, however, of comparing the Federal Republic with Nazi Germany is highly questionable.

Michael Eben, in a continuation of Ziolkowski's analysis of Böll's religious symbols, concentrates on the aesthetics of bread and the communion of the meal in *The Lost Honor of Katharina Blum* and concludes that, although Katharina is not as religious a character as Leni, "the partaking of a meal is symbolic of the mutual affection and consideration of the participants" (Eben 1982, 265). With this view, Eben continues Durzak's interpretation of Böll's bread symbol in *The Bread of Those Early Years*. Unlike Durzak, however, Eben does not center his interpretation of the novella on this symbol alone.

As more and more German critical ideas entered the United States, fewer critics arrived at an outright rejection of Böll's works. As the understanding for German problems grew, even Nägele's and Conard's initiatives connecting Böll's experiences with those of American writers were taken up, thereby relating German and American social patterns. A good example of the new way of looking at Böll is evident in Joseph Hynes's essay on Böll and Salinger, written for the popular-fiction periodical *Novel:* Böll's *The Clown* is seen here as an important book for Western culture, a book that shows how "society might be able to solve its problems and get out of its own mess if it were willing and able to give up capitalistic free enterprise, organized religion, party politics, and other such institutional components of what we regard as Western culture" (Hynes 1990, 279). It appears that by the 1990s Böll was considered an author by Americans who could find a way out of commercialized Western culture.

3. Feminist literary criticism plays an important role in the United States, and since the protagonist in Böll's book *The Lost Honor of Katharina Blum* is a woman, and she is viewed as being politically aware, this book has been considered the most feminist of Böll's novels. Most feminist studies develop innovative ideas by combining a structural analysis with a content analysis, following the Durzak model. The British critic Moray McGowan tries to reflect on the political developments in the increasingly complex structure of Böll's novels. As a literary historian, McGowan relates Böll's image of the woman to images found in medieval courtly love or in a little known Anglo-Irish tradition. McGowan claims that Böll draws on the Irish motif of Cathleen ni Houlihan, which, "with its romantic associations of the struggle against an alien oppression, matches Böll's own attitude to West German society" (McGowan 1984, 226). McGowan's research is further proof of Böll's fascination with Irish history and supports the thesis that Böll saw life in Ireland as a romantic alternative to Germany's development in the 1950s.

Aleidine J. K. Moeller analyzes the development of female figures in Böll's work and comes to the conclusion that Böll's women have become increasingly assertive and that with *Group Portrait With Lady* and *The Lost Honor of Katharina Blum,* women cease being merely the catalysts for their male partners (Moeller 1979, 1987). Although not a pronounced feminist, Moeller nevertheless asserts that a thorough examination of the female figures is essential for understanding Böll's fiction.

Evelyn T. Beck, in her decidedly Marxist interpretation, could be considered the first truly feminist literary critic with her attacks on Böll's female figures in *The Clown.* Her perceptive approach takes Böll's ideology apart, and she states that in his treatment of women he "idealizes the inferior roles dictated to women by men" ("[Böll] idealisiert die untergeordnete Rolle, die der Frau zudiktiert worden ist"; Beck 1984, 60). She also assails the difference between Marie and Hans as an arrogant reflection of the existing power structure since the man does not lose anything through premarital sex, while the woman loses everything. According to Beck, Böll can look at the world only through a man's eyes. His women are not real; he sees them only as idealized angels and helpers to support the man's "important" position. Beck's article reflects a belief that became widely popular in radical American feminism during the 1980s. Similarly, Margareta Deschner considers Böll's feminism idealistic and utopian, since women have to make up for men's deficiencies through their "holistic" nature. Women, Deschner concludes, represent Böll's romantic belief in the wholeness of nature; they affirm the "unity of all life" (Deschner 1985, 126).

Irene Compton is not as harsh on Böll when she considers Böll interesting to feminists because he was working toward emancipation of both men and women. Compton admits that Böll's feminism is traditional and derived from his perception of his mother, Maria Böll, more than any other influence (Compton 1987, 20). James Henderson Reid agreed with Compton's observation that Böll's feminism "was to a large extent born out of indignation at the upbringing of his mother, the way she as a woman was deprived of educational opportunities" (Reid 1988, 16). Compton admits that female figures in Böll's earlier books are depicted in traditional terms, as helpers to the male protagonists. However, Böll viewed the working women of the war years as fellow victims of World War II. Mirroring developments in German society during the economic recovery period, Böll's women regress to inaction in his later works. Compton thus argues that Böll saw the developments of his times with regard to women's emancipation as regressive. As the entire society regressed, so did these women living with the conservative social developments since 1950. The women in Böll's last novels, *The Safety Net* and *Women in a River Landscape*, have taken up the traditional practices and rules of staying at home and taking care of the house instead of learning from the experience of the war (Compton 1978, 40). Although women are now better educated and more able than ever to enter the workforce, the author's female protagonists are again in the home nurturing and supporting their families. Compton does not criticize Böll's writing; instead she affirms his ability to write perceptive realism even aside from his political beliefs. Compton supports Böll's idealistic vision of the "new woman" who must be able to change society through her female characteristics. However, at the same time, this ideal woman should never lose her feminine appeal, but should create a comfortable home for her family, since only as a "human woman or as a female human (these terms are exchangeable for Böll) can she represent a more human position in life" (Compton 1987, 73).[1]

An important feminist initiative came from Charlotte Armster, who claims that due largely to male-initiated literary criticism, "the sexual nature of 'lost honor' and its connection to violence, as implied by the interplay between title and subtitle, was simply overlooked" (Armster 1988, 84). The honor concept refers to eighteenth-century ideas of bourgeois emancipation from the aristocratic ruling class that Lessing and Schiller had explored in their plays *Emilia Galotti* and *Kabale und Liebe*. Armster also refers to Schiller's novella *Der Verbrecher aus verlorener Ehre*, although we know that Böll repeatedly denied a deliberate connection between the two texts. Armster expands the eighteenth-century honor-concept to that of the female body by claiming that the idea of lost honor is a concept denoting a loss of virginity when applied to women. In this manner, Armster shows how this two-hundred-year-old concept could still become instrumental for the emancipation of a twentieth-century woman. Although Armster follows Böll in explaining Katharina's image as nonviolent nun, an image that is "diametrically opposed to the one formed by the police and Tötges," Armster still condemns Katharina's act of violence in the novel as ineffective since it "cannot redeem her public name" and cannot challenge the sexual stereotypes that Böll used to create his character. However, the potential for effective political action was there, as Armster confirms in her otherwise sharp criticism of the novella.

4. A major reassessment of Böll's work took place after his death in 1985, both in Germany and in the United States. In his short obituary in the *German Quarterly*, the German poet-critic Walter Höllerer emphasized Böll's ability to alert his readers to the constant dangers lurking behind the calm facade of the forty-year "peace" in Europe (Höllerer 1986, 103). Unlike the German Höllerer, the British critic Keith Bullivant did not feel the need to hide his reservations toward

---

[1] ". . . denn nur als menschliche Frau bzw. als fraulicher Mensch (diese beiden Begriffe sind für Böll austauschbar) kann sie die Überbringerin einer humaneren Lebenshaltung sein."

Böll, who "frequently dances on the edge of cloying sentimentality or rather heavy symbolism that are at variance with his otherwise economical and perceptive realism" (Bullivant 1986, 248). Bullivant is also less forgiving of Böll's political reservations toward the Federal Republic when he notes that Böll "did at times seem blind to the many admirable features of the Republic, particularly when compared to other Western democracies, features which give us our essentially positive attitude to that country" (Bullivant 1986, 247). Bullivant's moderate reaction to Böll's literature may well be representative for the majority of readers and critics in the Anglo-Saxon world who grew up with stable political systems and cannot understand the political zeal of their German colleagues, especially Marxists. Since Bullivant is a professor of German literature, he may have perceived his objections as representing the interests of his British students of German who should not learn about political subversion in Germany; Bullivant, like most teachers of German culture abroad, wants his students to appreciate "modern" Germany. The teacher of German culture who operates outside of Germany sees his efforts of setting up a positive image of Germany endangered by Böll's approach to German culture. Here the complicated political situation that Böll faced in his Anglo-American reception becomes clearer; in order to understand Böll's political criticism of Germany's social conditions, Germany itself has to be understood first. An outsider to German political affairs, whether American, British, or a citizen of any other country, has little information about Germany other than the preconditioned image and usually does not want to get involved in Germany's internal political affairs. Therefore, for a foreign reader of Böll's work, it is simply easier to concentrate on the novel form rather than the involved, subversive political criticism of Germany.

In his review article on *Women in a River Landscape*, Bullivant is one of the very few critics to find something positive to say about that book, which he considers "a modern morality play in novel form" (Bullivant 1986, 249). By using a historical method of intertextuality, Bullivant can concentrate on "human values or failings" embodied in the various characters in this morality play. Although the novel is thus elevated beyond the political discussion, Bullivant does not close his eyes to the fact that it is a book about a specific moral dilemma, "the moral choice facing the society in which the novel is located" (249).

Similarly, his countryman James Henderson Reid gives a positive judgment of Böll's *The Safety Net*. Reid attributes the "capriciousness" of the critical reaction to the novel in West Germany to the "journalistic nature of . . . giving an instant judgment on the basis of a single reading of the novel" (Reid 1983, 126). He wants to correct the current negative West German perception represented by Schütte's statement that Böll's "progression" (*Fortschreibung*) becomes "regression" (*Rückschreibung*; Schütte 1974). In his reappraisal, Reid maintains that *The Safety Net* is thematically related to Böll's recent works — for example, in exploring the role of women in society — but the book also continues issues like power and corruption which preoccupied Böll since his earliest days. In form, *The Safety Net* "seems more closely similar to the works of the 1950s, especially *Billard um halbzehn*" (Reid 1983, 134). Like *Billiards*, *The Safety Net* is told as a third-person narrative from the restricted perspective of one of the characters in indirect interior monologue. Reid maintains that "the main purpose of the technique is to represent a formal equivalent of the isolation in which the characters are living, an isolation which is itself a function of the political situation in which they find themselves" (138). Thus Reid demonstrates how Böll was using at the end of his life techniques similar to those he had used at the beginning of his career.

Reid's 1988 book *Heinrich Böll: A German for His Time* summarizes the results of yet another decade of Böll research in England and America, just as Schwarz had reflected a sense of the 1960s and Conard the 1970s. The book is an expansion of Reid's 1973 book *Heinrich Böll: Withdrawal and Re–Emergence*, a title which indicates his interest in critical "thematic continuation" similar to Böll's own program of continuous development of his literary themes (*Fortschreibung*). The 1988 book will be reviewed here, since the first part of the 1973 book was incorporated with modifications into the later work. In the former book, Reid had described the narrative structure of Böll's works as "based not on plot, time and character, but on montage and leitmotiv," as shown in Böll's best book, *Billiards at Half-Past Nine* (Reid 1973, 34). *Billiards* was to Reid both a *nouveau roman* and its opposite, "for implicit in the novel's ending is an attack on the abstract, purely artistic existence which Robert has been leading" (Reid 1973, 57). Since any symbolic or narrative coherence was lacking in *Group Portrait With Lady*, he found this book "a much more rambling novel than anything Böll had written previously" (Reid 1973, 72). Since Reid had then not yet developed a theoretical reference system for Böll's work, his first book appears more superficial in its critical method.

Reid's 1988 book is an intellectual tour de force combining formal and social criticism in an excellent manner. Reid now recognizes Böll's specific German heritage when he writes that Heinrich Böll was an intellectual of the Continental rather than the British variety. And due to the different social context, many of the controversies Böll described in his books would be "unlikely in a British context, simply because British writers do not usually intervene in the day to day business of politics" (Reid 1988, 4). Here the British critic Reid makes an honest attempt to place Böll in the Continental-European, here, German context and judge him by Böll's own standards rather than applying Anglo-American criteria. In other words Reid positions himself as an outsider rather than making Böll the outsider. From this point he can develop excellent critical insights into Böll's fiction that Germans, especially, did not recognize and from which they should benefit.

Reid divides Böll's oeuvre into premodernist, modernist, and post-modernist periods. One of the central concepts of modernism was the autonomy of the work of art. (Such autonomy would later give way in *End of a Mission* to an attempt to combine art with life.) Reid claims that Böll's earlier works of the 1950s share many of the features of this kind of modernism. The absence of the overt narrator in *Billiards at Half-Past Nine*, who in premodernist (nineteenth-century) fiction acted as a bridge between the world of the text and the world of the reader, especially establishes this book as a highly modernist text. There are modernist elements in other texts by Böll, for example, in *Adam, Where Art Thou?*, in which montage is used as a modernist element. Another typical modernist perspective is introduced in *And Never Said a Word*, in which, according to Reid, "there is no indication of why, when or for whom [Käte and Fred] are writing" (Reid 1988, 98). Both Käte and Fred meet people independently; the girl in the café, for example, is described anew from Käte's perspective as if the reader had not already met her in a previous scene with Fred. Reid relates this formal aspect to the social background and observes, "there is no community of narrative, just as there is no community in their marriage" (98). Other modernist techniques can be found in several of Böll's novels and stories of the 1950s, such as the spatializing of time, which reduces narrated time and "creates an aesthetic pattern based on colours and leitmotivs." Another modernist element Reid lists is the avoidance of references to historical events and historical places in order "to disguise the fact that the novel is a construct within the reader's reality" (Reid 1988, 147). Böll's writing is less modernist than Arno Schmidt's and Wolfgang Koeppen's modernist prose experiments of the 1950s, and he has usually been regarded as a realist in the nineteenth-century tradition (84). However, despite this nineteenth-century premodernist touch, Böll's novels of the 1950s still bear many of the marks of modernism, a sort of provincial modernism, as practiced in West Germany when it was widely felt that German literature had to catch up with international developments from which it had been excluded by National Socialist policies. Böll's modest modernism was considered provincial and may explain some of the problems Böll had with international audiences where access to truly modernist texts had never been interrupted.

If Böll's techniques of the 1950s show a modest imitation of modernist styles, the 1960s witness a breakthrough to postmodernism with *Absent Without Leave.* and the "highly post-modern" *Group Portrait With Lady.* Despite Reid's labeling *Group Portrait With Lady* a postmodern novel, his impression of the book is surprisingly less favorable than that of other (minor) novels, due to the "slovenly" and unliterary style Böll employs in this book (178). However, Reid likes Böll's ingenuity in inventing an abundance both of characters and events. All of these features culminate, according to Reid, in Böll's *Lost Honor of Katharina Blum.* The careless language in *Katharina Blum,* heavily criticized by many, is, according to Reid, "a deliberate device to prevent the text becoming an aesthetic and therefore irrelevant artefact" (185) – the book is a return to premodern techniques of concentrating on substance over form. *The Safety Net* represents a return to the 1950s and is especially reminiscent of techniques Böll used in *Billiards at Half-Past Nine,* as Reid had shown in his earlier article. Böll used a similar modernist method in *Women in a River Landscape,* which, according to Reid, is a "baroque state action," as experimental as anything he had written, a modernist "dramatic" novel, "a parody of the cheap novelette, an elegy of contemporary Germany" (219). It is interesting to see that Reid's assessment of Böll's last book is almost identical with Bullivant's.

Presently, American critical approaches to Böll's work are almost identical with those in Germany: Anglo-American text-centered approaches are becoming more and more popular in Germany, just as the British and the Americans are discovering Germany's social history and applying it to literary texts. Therefore, when Schirrmacher attacks the entire West German literary tradition of the last forty years, he finds words of rejection equally strong in Britain, in America, and in Germany (Schirrmacher 1990). When Schirrmacher concludes that since the "old" Federal Republic has ceased to exist socially relevant writers like Böll do not represent anything now, he is refuted by critics such as Bullivant saying that "there has not been yet another 'Stunde Null,'" that in fact the Federal Republic has been expanded, and with it the importance of its history. Böll's work still constitutes an important part of German cultural history (Bullivant 1991). Böll has in fact become a respectable part of the now expanded and internationally more respectable Federal Republic, since more than any other writer Böll's literature reflects the forty-year history of the West German republic.

III. THE RECEPTION IN WEST GERMANY

A: From *Adam, Where Art Thou?* to *End of a Mission*

THE SUCCESS OF BÖLL'S BOOKS in West Germany came more slowly than in other countries, both in journalistic as well as academic reception. The first critical evaluations of Böll's early books, especially his short stories, were intended as aids in interpretation for classroom teaching. Consistent with the general atmosphere of the 1950s, reviewers were not at all interested in analyzing the recent political disaster, the Nazi era, but were looking for eternal values. Leo Lauschus, in his interpretation of "Traveler, If You Come to Spa . . .," is typical when he speaks of the "human helplessness in front of the extraordinary power of fate" ("die Nichtigkeit des Menschen gegenüber der ungeheuren Macht des Schicksals"; Lauschus 1958, 84). And Curt Hohoff analyzed the pistol symbol in "In the Valley of Thundering Hooves" ("Im Tal der donnernden Hufe") as "the negative Jerusalem, the hell of war, where demonic lust is at work" (Hohoff 1968, 196). Karlheinz Daniels was looking for another reality behind Böll's story, because true fiction, especially the short story, is characterized by its inclination to "transcend reality and offer references which point to something beyond this reality" (Daniels 1966, 31).[1] In his useful introduction to Böll's short stories in 1988, Bernhard Sowinski includes several good examples of these early attempts to interpret Böll's short stories in the "jargon of authenticity" ("Jargon der Eigentlichkeit"), an existentialist epithet taken from Heidegger's language. As an example for this approach, Sowinski singles out Motekat's almost incomprehensible interpretation of the short story "What a Business" ("So ein Rummel"), in which the female protagonist is supposed to represent a different world of invulnerability (Sowinski 1988, 58). In a similar interpretation, Anneliese Phlippen sees the woman in the same story as an unreal monster (Phlippen 1958). Sowinski reports that Böll became increasingly irritated with

---

[1] "... [die], den Rahmen einer wie immer gearteten Realität zu übersteigen und Bezüge auf[...]weisen, die auf ein Dahinterstehendes, Erkennbares oder Erahnbares weisen."

these inept attempts at interpretation by German schoolteachers in the 1950s and refused to read them.

However, press reviews and quickly written teacher manuals grew out of the general atmosphere of existentialist writing that became popular with Heidegger's existentialist jargon of "authenticity" (*Eigentlichkeit*). Klaus Jeziorkowski, one of Böll's first substantial critics, analyzed the short story "The Discarder" ("Der Wegwerfer") together with the later novel *Billiards at Half-Past Nine* according to the poetic rhythm they invoke. Jeziorkowski's methodological tools are clearly defined in the concentration on the narrative structure, and as a strict formalist, Jeziorkowski resists the temptation to interpret any theological and ideological aspects into Böll's symbolism (Jeziorkowski 1968, 161). Jeziorkowski shows how the novel *Billiards at Half-Past Nine* has a graphic design like that of the short story "The Discarder," which is structured by an "alinear curved line indicating time and dependent on the viewer's position . . . , as determined by Einstein's relativity theory" (Jeziorkowski 1968, 178).[1] These early existentialist interpretations were often so difficult to follow that they did not result in many followers except writers of the inadequate school manuals. Therefore academic publications on Böll remained scarce in West Germany, as evidenced in Werner Lengning's bibliography in Ferdinand Melius's introduction to Böll's work of 1959, which lists mainly the available press reviews on Böll (Melius 1959). In subsequent editions, Lengning developed his bibliography into one of the most comprehensive on Böll (Lengning 1968, 1972).

With the publication of *The Clown*, Böll's greatest success in Germany, press reviews abounded. The weekly *Die Zeit* decided to publish eight contradictory reviews, as the paper did not want to pass judgment on the book. *The Clown* was labeled the book of the decade, the way Grass's *Tin Drum* had been labeled the most important book of the 1950s. Eventually Böll's book produced a flood of academic publications. The first book-length study was written by Albrecht Beckel, a politician of Germany's Christian Democratic Union (CDU) and the mayor of the city of Münster, who felt Böll's political opinions needed correcting and wanted to vindicate Böll's Catholicism (Beckel

---

[1] ". . . von der alinearen, gekrümmten und zum Standort hin relativen Zeit . . . , wie sie die Einsteinsche Relativitätstheorie definiert."

1966). Beckel begins with the assumption that Böll wants to improve the relationship between the Catholic minister and his congregation; he furthermore (wrongly) assumes that *The Clown* is intended to activate lay ministers. Since he is inexperienced in analyzing literary texts, Beckel does not distinguish between statements that Böll made as an individual and those that he made in the fictional text; all that matters to Beckel is the fact that Heinrich Böll has a feeling heart and that he considers Böll to be a sympathetic person. Since Beckel is not a critic, he refers in his analysis to interpretations such as a review in *Der Spiegel* that attributed Böll's commercial success to his easy writing style and his tendency to present stories with a good ending; in other words, Beckel believes, as does the *Spiegel* reviewer, that Böll is a popular author, and he puts him more in the category of entertainment, rather than that of serious literature.[1] Beckel's analytical method follows Wolfgang Kayser's notion of textual interpretation as relating the text's meaning to its form; he analyzes the train symbol in *The Train Was on Time* as representing claustrophobia ("als Symbol des Eingeschlossenseins"; Beckel 1966, 40). Beckel's overall tendency is to rescue Böll as a Catholic writer from political attacks after the publication of *The Clown*. Böll, Beckel believes, is and will always be a writer who is primarily interested in supporting Christian issues which are centered in the family; he will always support traditional Western values (Beckel 1966, 67).

2. After this first book on *The Clown*, no major critical work on Böll was published for some time, which was partially due to the fact that Böll had not written any major work during the 1960s, and partially due to the literary establishment's lack of interest in the kind of aesthetic provocation Böll intended with his novels *The Clown* and *End of a Mission*. However, Böll's literature gained attention with the beginning of the student revolts at German universities, and some critics were now eager to make Böll appear as a forerunner of this movement; one could say in fact that Böll's reputation became estab-

---

[1] This popular notion of dividing literature into *Unterhaltungsliteratur* (*U-Literatur*) and *Ernste Literatur* (*E-Literatur*) was often used to denounce an author; that is what *Der Spiegel* in its slanted comments intended. However, Beckel does not follow this traditional division; he might not even be aware of it, and he treats Böll as a serious author.

lished in West Germany with the student movement in 1968. Reich-Ranicki's critical book partially fulfilled the expectations of the new generation, and because it was intended primarily as a birthday gift for Böll's fiftieth birthday, the editor was able to gather in his volume major voices of Germany's growing community of Böll admirers, among them several representatives of the fledgling Marxist community such as Georg Lukács and Theodor Adorno.[1] Others included Walter Jens, Siegfried Lenz, Carl Zuckmayer, Klaus Harpprecht, Carl Amery, Fritz Raddatz, Günter Gaus, Stefan Heym, Hildegard Hamm-Brücher, Ernst Fischer, Cesare Cases, and Martin Walser. The book is indeed a classic piece in the history of Böll reception and is still one of the most popular books on Böll due to its availability as a paperback. Because of the restlessness at German universities at that time, Reich-Ranicki wanted to emphasize revolutionary aspects in Böll's writings. Dieter Zimmer asserts that Böll was trying to find his own way to a political rebellion (Zimmer 1971, 209).

The majority of critics in this volume obviously support Böll's quest for revolt; two notable exceptions, Günter Gaus and Fritz Raddatz are not interested in analytical comments in their essays but use Böll to establish their own political positions, Gaus from a progressive Social Democratic position, trying to win Böll back to the SPD, and Raddatz from an aggressive Marxist position from which he rejects Böll as a renegade. Böll "only interpreted the world differently, after others before him had been able to change it," Raddatz quips, thereby reversing Marx's classic sentence. Raddatz objects to Böll's restraint toward "revolutionary practice" and knows that real revolutionaries should not pin their hopes on Böll (Raddatz 1971, 114).[2] Raddatz's attack, however, was later rebutted by Peter Schütt, a party communist of the DKP (German Communist Party), who claims that Raddatz changed his former liberal position under the pressure of the student revolt and distanced himself from Böll's more moderate position. The main purpose of Schütt's article, however, seems to be to align Böll with the Marxist cause in West Germany (Schütt 1975, 171).

[1] The book appeared originally in 1968 in Cologne with Böll's publisher Kiepenheuer & Witsch, and gained immense popularity in the subsequent dtv-editions since 1971. The following quotes are from the 1971 dtv-edition.

[2] "Heinrich Böll hat unsere Welt verschieden interpretiert, nachdem es anderen vor ihm gelang, sie zu verändern."

Schütt claims that Reich-Ranicki's and Raddatz's resentments against Böll are simply modified conservative resentments.[1] Schütt sets up his own political vision of a "people's front" (*Volksfront*) for the 1970s which must have had followers among neo-Marxists, and reasons that Catholic writers like Böll are still needed in all countries where Catholicism maintains positions of power. Schütt predicts for Böll a status in Germany similar to Heinrich Mann's in the 1920s when he activated parts of the bourgeoisie for the Marxist cause. Schütt's (and Raddatz's) political argumentation was the first in a long line that liberal intellectuals used to establish their own political viewpoints; the texts themselves seemed only an excuse for this battle.

While Fritz Raddatz established himself as a true revolutionary in Reich-Ranicki' book, Theodor Adorno demonstrated a more understanding position and praised Böll as a writer who broke away from the "disgusting German tradition which equates mental achievement with its affirmative character" (Adorno 1971, 8);[2] Böll, as a subversive writer, does not long for positions of power or recognition. And Georg Lukács, the éminence grise of orthodox Marxist literary criticism, praised Böll's work as being part of nineteenth-century literary traditions, which, coming from Lukács, was the ultimate compliment, since he had modeled his entire critical writing on nineteenth-century realist writing. Lukács praised Böll's literary figures as "typical" for their time and as attempting to overcome the animality of their existence; they are "masters of their own fate" – a model for realistic literature (Lukács 1971, 255). This official endorsement by a leading Marxist critic probably did more for Böll's work than many detailed discussions of his books. Other critics in this volume followed up on Lukács's ideas. Hans Egon Holthusen saw a connection between Böll's writings and Germany's social novel of the 1920s (Döblin), and a continuing tradition going back to Thomas Mann and Theodor Fontane. Joachim Kaiser, the critic from the *Süddeutsche Zeitung*, connected Böll to the Hölderlin tradition of compassion (Kaiser 1971, 51), and Carl Zuckmayer simply described *And Never Said a Word* as

---

[1] ". . . unzweideutig aus rechten Ressentiments gegenüber Bölls politischer Haltung und Wirkung."

[2] ". . . jener abscheulichen deutschen Tradition, welche die geistige Leistung ihrem affirmativen Wesen gleichsetzt."

one of "the most beautiful and worthwhile books written in the last fifty years" (Zuckmayer 1971, 52).

Just as Lukács pointed to Böll's convincing representation of the characters in his novels, so did Walter Jens and the novelist Siegfried Lenz. Jens pointed out that Böll's characters are not "master people" (*Herrenmenschen*), a popular label of the late 1960s that Willy Brandt would later apply to himself, but "little men" instead, victims of society (Jens 1971, 23). This emphasis on the underdog in society became the popular mode of storytelling during the "revolutionary" changes of the 1960s. Lukács's approach is employed by Cesare Cases in his famous analysis of "The Balek Scales" ("Die Waage der Baleks"), which is reprinted in Reich-Ranicki's book. The Balek family, Cases argues, is a prime example of capitalist exploitation (Cases 1971, 175). Despite several inconsistencies in Böll's historic depiction, Cases comes to the conclusion that the collective blindness of the people in Böll's story is our own blindness, thereby opening up the interpretation for contemporary application (Cases 1968, 178).

Since a good part of Böll's thinking centered around Catholicism, liberals like the *Spiegel* editor Rudolf Augstein found Böll's stories tasteless (Augstein 1971, 81). And Klaus Harpprecht criticized Böll for underestimating the power of the church and overestimating the power of the relatively young CDU (Harpprecht 1971, 86). Böll's fellow Christian Carl Amery explained Böll's political views as archaic in a positive sense, since he laments an element long since lost by the church, its power to stabilize society. According to Amery, Böll does not realize that the church has no power left to resist the drastic changes of our time (Amery 1971, 94).

Böll's political position was not only criticized by Marxists, as was to be expected, conservatives had something to say too. Although Reich-Ranicki did not invite many conservatives to contribute to his book, the language critic Dolf Sternberger was given an opportunity to explain his views. Although he admires Böll as a writer, he admits his confusion about Böll's political views, especially as expressed in the Wuppertal speeches, in which Böll states that as a writer he does not need any form of government, as a writer he is above the law. This romantic view is inexcusable to the pragmatist Sternberger, who shudders at the possible implications of such an anarchist viewpoint.

As a rationalist, Sternberger does not feel comfortable with Böll's utopian visions (Sternberger 1971, 103-8).

With his book Reich-Ranicki had not simply provided the breakthrough for Böll on the academic front but had also set the form for many books on Böll to come: a collection of articles on as many books and aspects of the author's work as possible by as many different writers of as many different political persuasions as possible. The major reason for this format obviously was that the editor wanted to show the broadest possible range of opinions, and to appeal to as many readers as possible. The popularity of this format is demonstrated by the large number of imitators it found: Lengning (1972), Arnold (1972), Grützbach (1972), Jurgensen (1975), Matthaei (1975), Beth (1975), and dell'Agli (1984), to cite the most important ones. In the late 1970s and the 1980s monographs rather than collections of essays dominated the scene.

In 1972 the second, greatly expanded, edition of Melius and Lengning's book was published; it introduced a variety of critics who had established themselves through newspaper reviews. Lengning's intention differs drastically from Reich-Ranicki's in avoiding political discussions altogether; he concentrates instead on stylistic and structural approaches. In one of the key essays of this volume, Karl August Horst points out similarities in the treatment of time between *Billiards at Half-Past Nine* and the French *nouveau roman*. Horst states that French novels do not relate events that follow each other; instead, they "present a closed space for the imagined simultaneity of disjointed events" (Horst 1972, 77).[1] This explains why Robbe-Grillet's noveltechnique has little in common with a psychological novel; it reduces literature to mathematical abstractions, the same way Böll's novel lacks psychologically convincing characters. The critic Karl Korn, however, prefers this method to Böll's later psychological realism, and reassessing Böll's oeuvre in the light of *Billiards*, he finds it to be on the highest level. Since Böll does not treat the characters in his novel as individuals, he can concentrate on historic events, "like a literary archaeologist who uncovers the social layers going back to the Roman roots" (Korn 1972, 107). Urs Jenny admires *Absent Without*

---

[1] "Man läßt, indem man das zeitliche Nacheinander relativiert, für die imaginäre Gleichzeitigkeit auseinanderliegender Vorgänge den geschlossenen Raum einstehen."

Leave, which he calls "a prose capriccio in the vein of Laurence Sterne and William Faulkner" (Jenny 1972, 93). Günter Blöcker compares *The Clown* with Salinger's *The Catcher in the Rye* and the Western tradition of the angry young man (Blöcker 1972, 89). With all of the essays in his book Lengning demonstrates how Böll's work is firmly grounded in Western traditions. Even when the authors in this volume discuss moral issues, they do not point out revolutionary aspects in Böll's work but rather ask, as Jean Amery does, whether Böll might not be the moral conscience of his country, or point out, as does Henri Plard, that Böll's work shows the "healing powers of human love" and of humility and courage (Plard 1972, 74).

Heinz Ludwig Arnold's collection of essays combines a discussion of social and moral issues in Böll's novels with a discussion of formal aspects (Arnold 1972, 2d ed. 1974). Arnold believes that Böll is the champion of post–World War II German literature and that especially with his short stories, he influenced numerous younger writers. The first volume of this *text + kritik* edition concentrates on the reception of *The Clown*, which, according to Arnold, will become a classic for "materialistic literature historians" about the Federal Republic (Arnold 1972, 2).[1] Heinz Hengst is interested in Böll's Catholicism and asks whether the combination of the law and mercy in both novels, *Billiards at Half-Past Nine* and *The Clown*, did not create "a new fictitious church by rematerializing the sacraments" (Hengst 1972, 25). However, Böll, as well as his clown Schnier, came to realize that this re-creation is ineffective (Hengst 1972, 25). Arnold's collection became famous for Jochen Vogt's indictment of "literary pedagogues" who abused their literary skills in interpretations for young students. What irks Vogt more than anything else is the tendency of these interpretations to subtract the social context from the stories and look for more "general human values" ("allgemeinmenschliche Werte"). None of these interpretations, Vogt claims, could match the brilliance of Cesare Cases's dialectical interpretation. Vogt also complains that these interpretations left out all those works by Böll that were important in understanding him as a social critic, for example all of his novels, "which made him famous worldwide" (Vogt 1972, 35).

---

[1] "Vermutlich wird, wenn später einmal die materialistischen Literaturgeschichts- schreiber die Geschichte von Staat, Gesellschaft und Kultur dieser Bundesrepublik schreiben, gerade dieser Roman eine hervorragende Stellung darin einnehmen."

Vogt expands on his charges later in articles and his book (Vogt 1978, 1987).

3. Manfred Durzak, a West German academic critic, established himself as a rival to Hans Joachim Bernhard's approach in East Germany with his *Habilitationsschrift* on the contemporary West German novel (Durzak 1971, 19-107). Durzak argues from a dialectical perspective similar to Bernhard's, but in order to distinguish himself from Bernhard, he is more critical and rejects several of Böll's works for formal inconsistencies. In his argument, Durzak rejects the East German notion of characterizing Böll's work as a literary resistance to the West German welfare state (Durzak 1971, 7). According to Durzak, Bernhard's interpretation is a complete misreading of Böll's intentions, since Böll is not a social revolutionary, nor should his technique be labeled socialist realism, although there are admittedly some similarities. On this account, Durzak argues, Böll's work could not be and never will be popular in the sophisticated United States, where people are afraid of any connection with socialism. Durzak argues that "in the Anglo-Saxon world the reception is less dominated by plot than by formal categories" (7). Since Durzak's interest is obviously more in Böll's popularity in the West than in the East, he cautions us against an author who is so readily accepted by Eastern European Communist readers. It seems as if there might be something seriously wrong with Böll's perception, namely his inability to recognize his own contradictions. This inability results in a readiness to accept situations as given, a "blindness to reflection" ("Reflexionsblindheit"); in other words, Böll lacks "a consistent position" ("einheitliche Haltung"; Durzak 1971, 20). Durzak is particularly bothered by Böll's inability to understand the political dubiousness of the petit bourgeoisie, whereas Günter Grass understood these conditions very well. Durzak's line of reasoning is often hard to follow since he judges Böll's literary production from an ambiguous standpoint wavering between neo-Marxist terminology and an attempt to please the "Anglo-American literary taste."

Durzak admires Böll's war novels for their unabashed moral standpoint but dislikes *And Never Said a Word*. "The book," Durzak writes, "seems like the compromise of a critical author, hard to justify," full of sentimentality that covers up antagonisms (47). It shows poor design and fails in combining both content and structure; the structure seems superimposed to the story, combined with an artificially unpretentious language – a completely failed novel. Durzak's aggressive condemnation of this book may be grounded in his frustration with Böll's political course in the early 1950s.

In stark contrast, Durzak admires *The Bread of Those Early Years* as a masterpiece; he is the only critic with such an extremely positive opinion. He regards the bread symbol as perfect for the postwar situation in Germany, since it incorporates various levels of reality. The carefully chosen language adds to the artistic achievement of this book, since it is the "climax of a carefully orchestrated novel, which makes this text one of the most complete prose pieces of the early Böll" (60). Durzak sees *Billiards at Half-Past Nine* as another major achievement in Böll's writing, since the characters in the novel can actively participate in history, while in earlier books his characters had been passive. Since the focus is on the family, the book is an attempt to use the family as salvation for society's ills. However, Durzak criticizes the buffalo sacrament as an "artificial symbol" that appears attached to the story. As Durzak sees it, the formal experimentation cannot overcome the thematic inconsistencies, which seems to be Böll's general problem.

However, in *The Clown* Böll returns to a more immediate approach. Like other critics (Sokel 1967, quoted in Perraudin 1988), Durzak regards Schnier as embodying marionettelike qualities as Kleist had described them in his essay on the marionette theater (Durzak, 84). In this interpretation the clown would represent the elevated state of the human mind that is needed to understand human life – a degree of sophistication, however, which eventually kills the artist in him. This level of sophistication would indeed explain Schnier's artistic failure, according to Kleist's theory. But despite his initial enthusiasm, Durzak worries about the ambiguous reception of the book, something he regards as a serious flaw of the book itself. Durzak clearly overestimates the power of the critic and bases his judgment on the book's reception. This book is only the final evidence in Durzak's argument that Böll as a writer is usually critically wrong in his political perception, which does not speak well of "the poetic abilities of the much acclaimed author" (Durzak, 96). Durzak sees clear evidence of this inability in *End of a Mission,* where the unintentional ambiguity is a result of Böll's incompetence:

> Despite a few perfect satirical highlights, and despite a new style appropriate to the story, *End of a Mission* gives us again the impression generally described as a general perception of the writer Böll, which now has turned into a permanent crisis. This crisis ultimately puts the poetic ability of the much acclaimed author Heinrich Böll in a bad light. (Durzak, 96)[1]

Durzak concludes that a certain uniformity of style might be found only in Böll's satirical consistency (Durzak, 384).

Böll's notion of the "rubber cell of art" ("Gummizelle der Kunst") may have been his own expression of the inability to connect art and life, perhaps too ambitious an undertaking. Böll realized that society also sees art as a "padded cell," and with this novel he wanted art and literature to be taken seriously by society. Böll wanted us to understand his novella as a way of using art as a means to protest current trends in politics and society, an aesthetic aim that is romantic and can be traced back to the dadaistic experiments of the 1920s:

> At that time I thought about the fact how the complete niceness of society toward art is really nothing more than a kind of padded cell. At the same time, I was reading about the provos in Amsterdam and their Happenings. I recognized that all art is taken seriously by this bewildering and incomprehensible society. This recognition got me thinking that art, that is, a Happening, is perhaps the last chance to break out of this padded cell; it can become a time bomb or the way to take the director of this madhouse out of action with poisoned chocolate candy. I decided on a combination of poisoned chocolates and a time bomb.[2]

---

[1] "Trotz einiger gelungener satirischer Höhepunkte, trotz eines von der Sache her legitimierten – für Böll – neuen Stils hinterläßt auch *Ende einer Dienstfahrt* jenen Eindruck, den man in der Literaturkritik in der Regel als Krise des Schriftstellers Böll beschreibt, nur daß es sich offensichtlich um eine permanente Krise handelt, die letztlich gegen die schriftstellerischen Möglichkeiten des vielgerühmten Autors Heinrich Böll spricht."

[2] "Um diese Zeit auch dachte ich besonders über die Tatsache nach, daß die komplette Nettigkeit der Gesellschaft der Kunst gegenüber ja nichts anderes als eine Art Gummizelle ist. Gleichzeitig las ich über die Provos in Amsterdam, las über Happenings, und die Erkenntnis, daß alle Kunst von dieser so fassunglosen wie unfaßbaren Gesellschaft ernst genommen wird, brachte mich auf die Idee, daß Kunst, also

With *End of a Mission*, he may have identified with the student revolts of the late 1960s, when students were trying to shake up society through political "happenings" similar to that presented in the novel. Böll's intention had been to show that the ruling class understands the danger of the Gruhls' political action and decides to cover it up. He also wanted to show the sympathy of the village people, who all understand and support the action. Most critics such as Durzak, however, did not see the intended political time bomb. Karl Migner supported Durzak's view of *End of a Mission* when he stated that the protest remained in the end unpolitical and individualistic (Migner 1970, 296). However, Jochen Vogt might be correct in asserting that the sympathetic support of the townspeople in the novel constitutes too much of a sense of idealized "home" (*Heimat*) as Böll had described it in his Frankfurt lectures; it excludes a reader from a different background. It is the atmosphere in Kleist's play *The Broken Jug* (*Der zerbrochene Krug*): provinciality.

4. Durzak's frequent skeptical references to Wolfgang Kayser's *Das sprachliche Kunstwerk* show what methodological school Durzak belonged to and the general dilemma of German Studies at the end of the 1960s and the early 1970s, when critics tried to apply the old terminology to the new social demands on literature. As a representative of the new generation, Durzak was interested in addressing social problems in literature – however, due to his aesthetic training, he rejected many of Böll's books as aesthetically inadequate. This transition from form-oriented approaches to dialectical political thinking in literature was something that many critics had to work out at this time. Like most of the form-oriented reviewers, Therese Poser was attracted to *Billiards at Half-Past Nine*, Böll's stylistically densest text. She came to the conclusion that the characters in *Billiards* are not meant to be realistic, but to represent something else, and they therefore depend on their function in the novel. Therefore, Poser writes, it is enough for the author to portray the characters with a few phrases that are repeated as a leitmotif: the words "correct, always correct"

---

auch Happenings, eine, vielleicht die letzte Möglichkeit sei, die Gummizelle durch eine Zeitzünderbombe zu sprengen oder den Irrenhausdirektor durch eine vergiftete Praline außer Gefecht zu setzen; ich entschied mich zu einer Kombination von vergifteter Praline und Zeitzünderbombe" (Böll, Heinrich. *Aufsätze, Kritiken, Reden.* Cologne: Kiepenheuer & Witsch, 1967, 264-65).

("Korrekt, immer korrekt") or Robert and Johanna's repeated words "the world is bad, there are so few pure hearts" ("Die Welt ist böse, es gibt so wenig reine Herzen"; Poser 1972, 252). From this reading it is only a small step for Poser to conclude that *Billiards* is really a political novel, and that it does not operate in a closed circle but is part of a political game to be uncovered by the reader. When Robert no longer orders his breakfast, the reader understands with the protagonist "that the myth has become senseless and that reality enters its place" (Poser 1972, 246). Michael Kretschmer employs a social-critical method and rejects Böll's abundant use of symbols, since Böll simply creates a new "artificial" myth to replace the traditional mystification of society as a metaphysical community of fate (with religion or a notion of nation). As a result, Böll represents a world through a "selected reality" as a "mythologized everyday world" ("eine mytho-logisierte Alltagswelt"; Kretschmer 1977, 212). Kretschmer rejects Böll's Romantic notion of the autonomy of the author's conscience, since the author has no right to create myths with his writing, just as the government has no right to mythologize our daily life through a notion of nation, or through a flag or any other symbol. Kretschmer advocates a stark realism and demands a style without symbols from writers in order to understand the political message.

In 1975 the Australian Germanist Manfred Jurgensen edited a collection of essays about Böll that should be included in this section on West German critical writing, since it summarizes very clearly its tendencies. As an outsider, Jurgensen does not want to take sides in the discussion about dialectical methods in Germany and therefore includes as many different views as possible. Jurgensen includes three essays from Marxists (two by Wirth, and one by Bernhard) along with Raddatz's "Eleven Theses" ("Elf Thesen"), and one essay each by a British, a French, and a Brazilian Germanist. This volume resembles Reich-Ranicki's book but shows how the entire approach toward Böll has become more political by 1975 compared with the 1960s (Jurgensen 1975). In one of the simplest essays, the West German Hinck bluntly declares that *The Clown* is a parable of the powerless political opposition in the "Bonn Republic," where Schnier expresses the opposition's blues in his song "Poor Pope John": these were the parallels (and simplifications) that readers wanted their critics to extract from literary texts in their vulgar-Marxist approaches (Hinck

1975, 23). Other than that, this book is a useful introduction into Böll scholarship, and other essays in this volume will be discussed more thoroughly in the following chapters.

B: The Discussion about *Group Portrait With Lady*

1. In 1971 Böll published his longest and most complex book, *Group Portrait With Lady*. When the Swedish Academy awarded him the Nobel Prize for Literature in 1972, it especially mentioned this novel in its dedication document. Although Böll had often been a nominee for the Nobel Prize, it is safe to say that had *Group Portrait* not appeared in 1971, Böll probably would not have received the award. The publishers called the book Böll's "most comprehensive, encompassing work," a "summation of his previous life and work," a view that was eagerly taken up by the critics.[1] The novel struck a responsive chord during the years of student protests when students were trying to create a "utopian" political world. Just as the students were being attacked by the traditionalists in Germany, Leni's openness to the victims of society was criticized by her relatives as unhealthy and destructive to the capitalist system. Böll clearly intended to portray in Leni a woman "who carried the whole burden of German history" ("die die ganze Last dieser Geschichte . . . auf sich genommen hat").[2]

Geno Hartlaub praised Böll's skillful technique of composing the novel and dismissed negative critiques as coming from those who as a matter of principle do not like fictive documentation literature altogether (Hartlaub 1971, 793). And Paul Konrad Kurz considered this novel the best Böll ever published; he did not limit his praise to the epic construction but praised the moral intention as well (Kurz 1971, 789). As in his interpretation of *Billiards*, Karl Korn also explained the complex structure of *Group Portrait* with Böll's intention to show us

---

[1] In the text on the dust jacket for both the German and the American editions (*Gruppenbild mit Dame: Roman*. Cologne: Kiepenheuer & Witsch, 1971; *Group Portrait With Lady*. Trans. Leila Vennewitz. New York: McGraw-Hill, 1973).

[2] "Heinrich Böll / Dieter Wellershoff: *Gruppenbild mit Dame*. Ein Tonbandinterview." *Akzente* 18 (August 1971) 331. Reprinted in *Die subversive Madonna: Ein Schlüssel zum Werk Heinrich Bölls*. Ed. Renate Matthaei. Cologne: Kiepenheuer & Witsch, 1975. 141.

the "archaeology of Cologne's society," especially of the lower classes. Böll, however, never worked from a master plan but rather developed his stories from his characters, as has been discussed.

Most of the criticism of *Group Portrait* concerns its structure. Reich-Ranicki declared the entire composition of this novel irrational, and emphasized he was not ready to wait for academic critics to take their time in proving the opposite:

> Should academic critics, who will definitely like to analyze *Group Portrait* (it is excellently suited for interpretations), conclude that the composition of the whole is well thought out and possibly refined, then I should be permitted to say right now that I will not believe any of it. There is absolutely no principle of organization to be seen in this book. (Reich-Ranicki 1971; 1979, 105; 1986, 60) [1]

This sentence is more revealing of Reich-Ranicki's method than it is a criticism of the book.

Reich-Ranicki's review of *Group Portrait* set the tone for many critical reviews. He liked this book even less than *The Clown* and overtly showed his dislike of the key character Leni by attacking her for her stupidity. Moreover, Böll's intended model of a sensitive socialist failed completely according to Reich-Ranicki:

> This Leni G. is not the least representative or typical for the represented period of our century. She is timeless and eternal. But what is being celebrated here is not the eternal Feminine but – and unfortunately that must be said with all respect for Böll – the apparently eternal German kitsch. (Reich-Ranicki 1971; 1979, 104; 1986, 61)[2]

Reich-Ranicki believed that Böll's language became sloppier as his books got longer, obviously too long for the writer to manage. Never

---

[1] "Sollten jedoch Wissenschaftler, die sich des ‚Gruppenbildes' bestimmt gern annehmen werden – es eignet sich vorzüglich für Interpretationen –, etwa zu dem Ergebnis kommen, die Komposition des Ganzen sei durchdacht und womöglich raffiniert, dann gestatte ich mir schon jetzt zu sagen, daß ich davon kein Wort glaube. Ein Formprinzip ist in diesem Buch überhaupt nicht erkennbar."

[2] "Diese Leni G. ist nicht im geringsten repräsentativ oder typisch für die dargestellte Epoche oder für unser Jahrhundert. Sie ist zeitlos und ewig. Aber was hier Urständ feiert, ist nicht etwa das Ewig-Weibliche, sondern leider – und das muß bei allem Respekt vor Böll doch ganz deutlich gesagt werden – der offenbar ewige deutsche Kitsch."

before had a major German writer dared to write in such a manner, and Böll made no linguistic distinction between characters; they all speak the same colloquial German. Other reviewers were less critical of the book, however. Jürgen Petersen supported Reich-Ranicki's observation, although he was more generous when he called the Leni figure "a synthetic figure, a personified idea, an idealistic existence" (". . . eine synthetische Figur, eine personifizierte Idee, eine idealistische Existenz"; Petersen 1971, 139) and understood the novel as "elevated poetic" reality with "a certain distance" from the prosaic reality surrounding us ("überhöht[e] Wirklichkeit, entrückt . . . in eine gewisse Distanz"; Petersen 1971, 141).

Durzak updated his book in 1972 with an article on *Group Portrait With Lady*. Durzak starts his dialectical interpretation with the structure and symbolism of the novel and comes to the conclusion that the individual parts of the novel do not fit together in a functional sense, and worse, they often contradict each other (Durzak 1972, 191). The only evident structuring device is the book's fictitious author ("auth."), whose task becomes more and more herculean. Durzak comments with cynicism on Böll's evident difficulty with holding the parts of the book together. Böll's book, Durzak claims, identifies and illustrates very clearly Böll's own political opinions, which should be hidden in a great work of art. In comparing Böll's fictional documentation with an American model, Truman Capote's *In Cold Blood*, Durzak complains that Böll does not stick to the category of the documentary, as opposed to the literary text, as Capote does; this text is, according to Durzak, just another example of Böll's confused thinking. Like Reich-Ranicki, whose review Durzak uses to substantiate his argument, Durzak finds much to criticize in Leni's character, since she is a literary figure who would not exist in any "empirical reality; she is the epiphany of pure humanity" (". . . empirische Wirklichkeit, . . . die Epiphanie vorbildlicher Mensch-lichkeit"; Durzak 1972, 193). Durzak explains how Böll composed his figures around Leni's character, as she "rests in her own sphere, complete like a monad" (Leibniz's autonomous "cell"; RZ), and it is the task of the fictitious author ("auth.") to remove the layers of historic and social reality as he would remove debris. Durzak comes to the cynical conclusion that despite his utopian theories and his principle of "refusing achievement" (*Leistungsverweigerung*), "the secularized

Epiphany in its idyllic realization remains questionable"(197). Thus according to Durzak the fundamental weakness in Böll's art is his inability to see the world the way it really is.

In two more articles, Durzak extended his analysis of *Group Portrait With Lady* to *The Lost Honor of Katharina Blum* (Durzak, "Entfaltung" 1975; "Leistungsverweigerung" 1975). In Durzak's eyes, the book (and the character) *Katharina Blum* is a double failure. The book fails first as a political text, because it offers no realistic solutions. Also, Katharina's protest is essentially private and does not significantly impair the yellow press or its questionable practices. The romantic characteristics, Durzak writes, supersede the realistic and practical ones; Böll's notion of solidarity is a completely unreal notion. Blorna, Katharina's employer in the novel, is the prototype of a liberal German intellectual of the 1970s, and his political dimension is that of a "spontaneous-petty-bourgeois-romantic anarchist" ("spontan-klein-bürgerlich-romantischer Anarchist"; Durzak, "Leistungsverweige-rung," 83). Böll's idea of solidarity also fails because the "author's superiority" ("auktoriale Überlegenheit") with which the story commences, capitulates to the glaring lack of harmony between content and formal construction. This disharmony goes so far that the task of narration is relinquished at the end to the main protagonist herself. Durzak speaks of a "formal atomizing" of the narrative perspective and thus the "self-abandonment" of the novel (Durzak, "Enfaltung"; 1975, 40).[1] The author who becomes involved in the plot has the function of binding together the diverging elements in the plot, and Böll fails. Even if the book were a parody of the nonfiction genre, it would have too many inconsistencies. This is a grand failure, according to Durzak, not simply of the fictitious narrator of *The Lost Honor of Katharina Blum* but also of the author, who capitulates when faced with a task too ambitious for him. In a final essay Durzak summarizes his conclusions about the failure of Böll's various narrators, starting with *Billiards at Half-Past Nine*, going through the shorter novels of the 1960s, and ending with *Group Portrait With Lady* and *The Lost Honor of Katharina Blum*. Citing Wolfgang Kayser's definition of the fictive narrator as one who establishes formal and ethical unity,

---

[1] "Mit der Aufsplitterung einer bestimmten Erzählperspektive droht dem Roman eine formale Atomisierung und damit eine Selbstaufgabe."

Durzak concludes that Böll never achieved this goal in any of his texts (Durzak 1976, 155).

Durzak considered *Group Portrait With Lady* (Durzak, "Entfaltung" 1975) a complete failure, and so did Georg Just (Just 1975, 55-76). Just starts from the assumption that Böll's literary devices, like his use of fictional documentation, were intended to keep the reader at a distance. However, the intended distance from the story is virtually destroyed by the author's strong political opinions, which surfaces in most parts of the story. Just concludes that the book is nothing more than a document of the author's personal political opinion; it reads like a political pamphlet. The various "informers" used in this fictitious "documentation" do not really represent different opinions – the endless monologues of these characters show little stylistic variation and serve only as extensions of the author's own tirades. The book, then, is a parody of the documentary, not intentionally but simply by incompetence (Just 1975, 65). As a result of these frequent outbursts of personal opinion, the book has virtually no structure; and worse, it repeatedly disintegrates into idyllic scenes, whereas in public opinion the novel is regarded as being critical of society. It appeals to the views of the German petit bourgeois in the late 1960s, who might have believed with Böll that Germany should have remained unpolitical and neutral as a result of World War II. Just's verdict of *Group Portrait With Lady* is devastating; the book pretends to be critical but demands complete uncritical identification. Just contends that such a process does not help in emancipating the reader, if that had been Böll's intention. Thus Just concludes his essay by stating that

> Böll's proclaimed unity of morality and aesthetics is practiced by him as the dissolution of aesthetics to his morality. His "Aesthetics of the Humane" is in reality the negation of aesthetics altogether by a mental construct. The structure of his novel is identical to that of his ideology: the division of the world into good and evil. The only difference between him and popular novels is – its political pretentiousness. (Just, 72)[1]

---

[1] "Die von Böll proklamierte Einheit von Moral und Ästhetik wird von ihm praktiziert als Auflösung der Ästhetik in seiner Moral. Seine Ästhetik des Humanen ist in Wirklichkeit Negation der Ästhetik durch ein schönes Ideologem. Die Struktur seines Romans ist die seiner Ideologie: die Zweiteilung der Welt in Gut und Böse. Vom Trivialroman unterscheidet er sich – durch seine Prätention."

Just concludes that *Group Portrait* is not a piece of literature but rather a "personal document" and therefore should be interesting only for a biographer or Böll's psychologist.

Raoul Hübner regards the popularity of *Group Portrait* (a best-seller, with about 258,000 copies sold by 1974) not as a primarily aesthetic text. Hübner uses Anglo-American entertainment literature as a model and compares Böll's novel with British detective novels because, as Hübner claims, Böll's "auth." should be seen as a detective along the lines of British crime stories (Hübner 1975, 122). In looking at the way Böll places his characters as representatives of ideas, Hübner reads Böll's characters as real people and not as the abstractions Poser had claimed to find (Poser 1972). However, Hübner claims that Böll focuses on characters at the expense of ideas. Hübner's approach suffers from a basic misunderstanding of the art of writing that is characteristic of ideological interpretations; these interpretations overlook that the process of writing originates in an authentic representation of characters and not in an urge to illustrate an abstract principle or idea through a character, as Hübner thinks. Criticizing character representations can thus serve as a test of how seriously a critic wants to understand the author's craft.

Hübner proceeds to connect Böll with fascism when he considers his rhenishness (*Rheinländertum*), a quasi-biologism copied from the Nazis' notion of race. Hübner further charges that *Group Portrait* is not a book about the real World War II but about unpolitical draft dodgers at the home front, a collection of petit bourgeois characters. In order to improve the reputation of these people, Böll elevates his petit bourgeoisie by labeling them proletarians, which was generally considered a more positive term.

Hübner labels Böll's vision of these would-be petit bourgeois anarchists romantic, and charges that it hardly differs from Ernst Kreuder's almost incomprehensible romantic scenario as depicted in Kreuder's novel *Hörensagen* of 1969, which Hübner called a religion of resistance. The only difference between Kreuder's novel and Böll's lies in Böll's referring more directly to the social context of the Federal Republic than Kreuder did with his more modernist approach, dispensing with concrete references. Hübner gleefully points out that Böll had written a positive review about *Hörensagen*, a novel about a fictitious drug that would make people more sensitive to art and nature. Since *Hörensagen* appeared at the height of the student revolts, Böll pointed out the connection between Kreuder's wonder drug and the long-haired students.[1] Thus Hübner comes to his final devastating conclusion: since Böll is a steadfast romantic with only fictional ideas and solutions, we should never be drawn into his world for possible solutions to real conflicts. He is unable to help solve any problems with his art (Hübner 1975, 143).

In her collection of essays on *Group Portrait*, Renate Matthaei collected the most significant works in Böll scholarship at that time: Hans Joachim Bernhard's essay about the character Leni, Manfred Durzak's article on the political dimension of *Group Portrait*, Victor Lange's essay about the history of Böll's narrative strategies, and Theodore Ziolkowski's famed essay about Leni's "beatification" process (Matthaei 1975), all of which have been discussed earlier in this book.

Arpád Bernáth gives a good analysis of *Group Portrait With Lady* in Matthaei's volume, in which he comes to conclusions similar to Reid's in his book on Böll; *Group Portrait* is a "post-crisis novel" that centers on both Böll's personal crisis and the crisis of the novel as a genre. However, the Hungarian Bernáth speaks only of a crisis of form in Western literature and at this point does not relate it to a crisis of capitalism in Western society (Bernáth 1975, 34). Bernáth especially points out that the past and the present are coming together in the structure of *Group Portrait*. Leni's continued sorrow over the loss of her lover Boris represents the continuation of the war in the present, which makes this Böll's "only real war novel," according to Bernáth. It also is a novel about the present situation in Germany, which Bernáth calls a *double novel* ("Doppelroman"; 39). Since Bernáth is interested in the continuity in Böll's work (he later gave a detailed report in Arnold's book on Böll; Bernath 1982), he shows how Leni's character represents a female Wilhelm Meister, the protagonist of Goethe's acclaimed nineteenth-century Bildungsroman. When Bernáth considers the development of Böll's female characters, he sees them all as one character and claims that Böll brought Marie back to Germany from Rome, where she had disappeared in *The Clown*. She is needed as an instructor for male Germans.

---

[1] (Heinrich Böll, "Untergrund im Widerstand," *Frankfurter Rundschau* 29 Nov. 1969; and in Christoph Stoll and Bernd Goldmann, eds., Ernst Kreuder: *Von ihm, über ihn.* (Mainz: V. Hase & Koehler, 1974): 68-70.

Both Matthaei and Balzer, who later became the editor of Böll's collected works, present Böll as an artist of the "utopia of unrepressed people" ("Utopie des entsublimierten Menschen"; Matthaei 1975, 8) or as a writer who creates a "sensual harmony of the citizens" ("Übereinstimmung auf sensualistischer Basis"; Balzer 1977, 29). Both argue along Böll's emancipatory lines. However, since Böll's concept is not completely rational, Balzer asks whether it should not be accepted as it is and whether literature might be perhaps a more suitable vehicle for a nonrational concept. His arguments completely contradict Hübner's straightforward rejection of Böll's artistic ideas and follow more along the aesthetic ideas that Friedrich Schiller developed during German Classicism that writers can create and explore a new idea through their aesthetic ability or play instinct (*Spieltrieb*).

Joachim Kaiser, a critic for the *Süddeutsche Zeitung* who has been a keen follower and supporter of Böll's work since the 1950s, sees Böll's work essentially along the same lines, claiming that the relationship between "aesthetic and nonaesthetic, that is nonfictional, reality is the real topic of the novel" (Kaiser 1978, 228).[1] What sounds like a compromise after the preceding debate is in fact an offer to regard Böll's book as an aesthetic experiment about the problem of writing itself. It is a novel about aesthetics in which Böll attempts to undo the eighteenth-century separation between intellectual and sensual perception; Leni is the focal point where this separation is overcome; she is an aesthetic construct holding together both concepts (228). Kretschmer had asked what would happen if the possibility of constructing a better world through literature were no longer possible (Kretschmer 1977, 212). What if we no longer had the possibility of attempting a solution to our present social problems, at least in play? If we follow Kaiser's (and Balzer's) arguments, Böll is not immersed in the Romantic tradition, but rather in the best tradition of Schiller's classical education. That seems to be the best possible (dialectical) compromise that could be reached by the end of the 1970s, and this

---

[1] "Geschichtlich gesehen versucht Böll, in der Sinnlichkeit Lenis die von der rationalistischen Philosophie des 18. Jahrhunderts vollzogene Trennung zwischen höheren und niederen Erkenntnisvermögen aufzuheben, indem er das in der Kunst kompensatorisch überhöhte, ästhetisierte Konkrete und Sinnliche wieder in seine wirklichen menschlichen Bezüge zurückführt."

still holds, since most subsequent interpretations follow Joachim Kaiser's lead.

C: The Political Battle of the 1970s

1. Böll was at this time turning away more and more from pure literature, and whatever the reasons were, he was becoming more involved in the political arena as a more directly involved political writer and journalist. He also accepted public offices and became the first German president of the International PEN Club in 1971. Since he became the official representative of German literature, many of his colleagues looked to him for leadership. Hans Werner Richter, the founder of Gruppe 47, for example, greatly admired Böll's international reputation with which he was able to achieve results "that we others cannot even dream of." In 1972, after the Christian Democrats attacked Chancellor Brandt's liberal *Ostpolitik*, Böll got directly involved in Brandt's successful reelection campaign. After Böll received the Nobel Prize for Literature in 1972, the first German writer after World War II to receive this award, his public reputation began to rise as he was praised by the Left as the "conscience of his age" and attacked from the Right as a writer without any real aesthetic values. Those opposed to Böll claimed that the best writers never received the Nobel Prize. Böll responded that, as a German, he could not afford not to accept the Nobel Prize, since Germany had not had many people whom the world could look up to after World War II.

In 1972 Böll published an article in *Der Spiegel* defending Ulrike Meinhof and the terrorist Baader-Meinhof Group against the premature conclusion of a mass-circulation daily, the *Bild Zeitung*, that the group was guilty. Böll's defense of Ulrike Meinhof is primarily emotional; it stems from a feeling that everybody in this society should be entitled to due process.[1] Böll spoke against the *Bild Zeitung*'s uncritical slander and maintained that former Nazis were being released from jail but that Ulrike Meinhof would find no mercy in such a political climate. In reaction to this article, the papers controlled by the conservative Axel Springer (who also owned the *Bild Zeitung*)

---

[1] "Will Ulrike Meinhof Gnade oder freies Geleit?" *Der Spiegel* 10 Jan. 1972.

published a letter written by Ministerpräsident Filbinger of the State of Baden-Württemberg and others asking for Böll's resignation as president of the International PEN. On June 1, 1972, Böll's house was searched by the police, and on June 7, in a debate in the West German Federal Parliament in Bonn, the Christian Democratic Union concluded, "fellow travelers" like Böll were more dangerous than the Baader-Meinhof group itself. It is no wonder that ideology superseded aesthetics in such an atmosphere and that Böll's supporters considered his political statements more important than his literary works.

The journalist Frank Grützbach summarized these events in a book, reprinting representative articles from several newspapers and journals. Grützbach found that the original discussion could have been completed in a week but that Böll's initial article was used over and over again as a vehicle to comment on other events (Grützbach 1972, 5). The conservative television moderator Gerhard Löwenthal viciously connected Böll to fascism in his obscure way:

> And the sympathizers of this leftist fascism, the Bölls and the Brückners [i.e., the Hanover professor who from the beginning had supported Böll and Ulrike Meinhof] and all the other so-called intellectuals are not a jot better than the spiritual trendsetters of the Nazis who once brought so much misery to our country. (Löwenthal in Grützbach 1972, 104)[1]

The reaction to the Meinhof article was Böll's initiation to the cruel political arena, and he was so antagonized by the conservative reaction to his plea for mercy that he decided never to open his mouth about this matter again (Grützbach 1972, 97). Günter Wallraff, his Cologne friend and co-author on several projects, sympathized with Böll's reaction to the attacks (Wallraff 1977/78, 6-7) and claimed that through his popularity Böll gave the Federal Republic moral credit abroad that Germany did not deserve. Karlheinz Göttert, who was arguing from a sociological point of view, saw this public conflict as an excellent example of how conflicts are resolved in the public sphere. Göttert shows in an elaborate model how spin-off conflicts

---

[1] "Und die Sympathisanten dieses Linksfaschismus, die Bölls und Brückners und all die anderen sogenannten Intellektuellen sind nicht einen Deut besser als die geistigen Schrittmacher der Nazis, die schon einmal so viel Unglück über unser Land gebracht haben."

were able to rekindle the original conflict weeks after the issues seemed to have been settled (Göttert 1980, 171). Another team of sociologists (Kepplinger, Hachenberg, Frühauf, 1984) divided the conflict into "four sub conflicts; 1. the original conflict and Böll's arguments in *Der Spiegel* with [the North Rhine-Westphalian Interior Secretary] Posser as the main opponent; 2. Böll's conflict surrounding [the Soviet dissident] Bukowski and Ulrike Meinhof, with [the conservative] Hans Habe as the main opponent; 3. the dispute surrounding the conservative charges that Böll was a 'salon anarchist,' with Frank Planitz as the main opponent; and 4. the conflict of describing Böll as 'sympathizer of leftist fascism and Nazi-sympathizer' with [the ZDF-commentator] Löwenthal as the main opponent" (Kepplinger, Hachenberg, Frühauf 1984, 159-60). The authors concluded, as had Grützbach earlier, that the dispute could have been resolved much earlier if other people involved had not used the publicity to generate interest in their own causes in which the author Böll eventually became a secondary feature.

2. Böll's literary response to these events was his book *The Lost Honor of Katharina Blum*, which appeared first in July 1974 in *Der Spiegel*. It was the first work of fiction ever published by the periodical. The first edition of the book, published in August of 1974, sold one hundred thousand copies in a few weeks and more than two hundred thousand by the end of the year. The paperback edition sold more than one million copies and was translated into eighteen languages.

The press reviews were extremely varied at first. Rolf Michaelis quipped in *Die Zeit* that Böll "went to the limits of what is convincing in literature. While [the newspaper man] Tötges ... is of course slimy (*schmierig*) and drives a Porsche, Katharina (her name comes from Greek 'the pure one') shines in a morally speckless 'Suwa-white' [a detergent], and of course she drives a used VW" (Michaelis 1974).[1] But there were others, such as Wolfram Schütte, who understood Böll and his protagonist Katharina in the tradition of the Austrian language

---

[1] "In der Idealisierung seines Blum-Mädchens geht Böll bis an die Grenze des literarisch Zulässigen und Überzeugenden. Während Tötges ... natürlich *schmierig* ist und Porsche fährt, strahlt die in einem gebrauchten VW kutschierende Katharina (griechisch: die Reine) in dem moralischen SUWA-Weiß . . . ."

critic Karl Kraus and who admired Katharina's linguistic sensitivity to distinguish between truth and falsehood. Schütte recognizes Katharina as a character deliberately constructed to change our perception of the German past. If Leni had been too fabricated a character, Böll wanted to show Katharina to be a prophetess as intuitive as Leni but more down-to-earth. Despite his basic agreement with Böll's fictional premise, the seer-character Katharina, Schütte nevertheless criticizes Böll's tendency to romanticize her and turn her into a female plebeian (Schütte 1974). It smacks too much of the mythologizing of the proletariat that had been popular during the 1920s and 1930s.

Dorothee Sölle is credited with giving the most reasonable assessment to both the Meinhof debate and Böll's *The Lost Honor of Katharina Blum* (Sölle 1974, 885-87). The main assumption of Sölle's review is the claim that Böll wrote a "realistic *1984*" for the Federal Republic, where the police is in charge of external control, and the press, especially BILD (Böll's novel version of the *Bild Zeitung*) is in charge of the internal control, of ideas and emotions as well as wishes (Sölle 1974, 886). Thus Katharina's rebellion is largely a linguistic resistance against a prescribed language where the sexual act can only be called *fucking* (*ficken*) and words like *kind* (*gütig*) are censored and replaced in the minutes with *very nice* (*sehr nett*) or *gentle* (*gutmütig*). Sölle's review seems to have captured the essence of Böll's book for the liberals very well, since it became one of the most quoted liberal essays in the ongoing debate.

Georg Stötzel, a sociologist, investigated Böll's vocabulary and came to the conclusion that Böll uses words differently from their commonly established meanings. The word *censorship* (*Zensur*), for example, has a different meaning in Böll's reference system than it generally does, and it is of little importance to Böll whether his use of the word is acceptable to the wider linguistic community (Stötzel 1978, 73). Thus the author acts like his protagonist when he has his own private vocabulary, and he, like Katharina, feels the need to preserve his language as an area of independence where nobody can or should interfere. Stötzel calls Böll's method a language-reflexive innovation ("sprachreflexive Innovation"). However, despite benevolent reviewers like Stötzel, many, especially well-known critics such as Walter Jens, complained about numerous linguistically botched passages ("sprachlich leider verunglückt"), and even Reich-Ranicki, in his otherwise praising review, lashes out at Böll's language.

3. One of the most quoted opinions in the conservative camp became Hans Habe's review (1974) of *The Lost Honor of Katharina Blum*. Since Habe had been in exile in the United States during the Nazi period and had fought against Hitler both as a soldier and as a journalist, he was free from the normal accusations from the Left equating conservatism with fascism. Thus he became one of the conservative front-line soldiers in the political battle of the 1970s and could say things that conservative opinion makers like Herbert Zehm, the editor of the conservative daily *Die Welt*, could not. Like Sölle and Stötzel, Habe criticizes Böll's use of language. However, Habe does not see Böll's style as the intended imitation of a bureaucratic police style. Habe looks at the stylistic awkwardness of the book as Böll's own inability; it exposes "his inability to love, his intellectual preaching [*Pharisäertum*], his inadequate logic, and his excessive judgment" (Habe 1974).[1] In America, Habe writes, somebody with Tötges's ability (the reporter who is killed by Katharina) would have received the Pulitzer Prize for his investigative reporting; in Germany someone with these abilities gets killed. This is indeed an interesting statement coming from Habe, who had actually worked in yellow journalism in Germany, Austria, and the United States since the beginning of his career; he obviously refers not to Tötges's sexual activities but to his investigative journalism and thus alludes to the provinciality of the Federal Republic. This provinciality was, according to Habe, largely the product of writers and intellectuals like Böll. The argument is interesting, since the perceived West German provincialism played a large role in the literary debate surrounding the novel *Was bleibt* by Christa Wolf in 1990 that was fueled by statements from Ulrich Greiner (in *Die Zeit*) and Frank Schirrmacher (in the *Frankfurter Allgemeine Zeitung*). Both debates, about *Katharina Blum* and about *Was bleibt*, have repeatedly been compared to each other and seem to reveal a feeling among critics of German backwardness that Germany still has to catch up with Western values.

---

[1] ". . . seine Unfähigkeit zu lieben, seinen Hang zum intellektuellen Pharisäertum, die Schwäche seiner Logik und die Maßlosigkeit seines Urteils . . . ."

On December 12, 1974, Karl Carstens, then chairman of the CDU/CSU delegation, demonstrated his ignorance about the *Katharina Blum* debate in the Bundestag: "I ask our people to distance themselves from terrorist activities, especially those of the writer Heinrich Böll who a few months ago wrote a book under the pseudonym 'Katharina Blum' that rationalizes the use of violence" (Balzer 1990, 6).[1] In 1972 Matthias Walden quoted Böll in a TV commentary as having described the West German constitution as a pile of manure (*Misthaufen*). Both parties went to court over this statement, Walden eventually losing the case after ten years, although he claimed in several interviews that he had never wronged Böll and that in fact he himself was correct in defending the Federal Republic against Böll's extremist opinions (Hill 1982; Walden 1982). When *The Lost Honor of Katharina Blum*, with its attacks on Springer's *Bild Zeitung*, became a nationwide best-seller, Springer's *Welt am Sonntag* discontinued publishing its weekly best-seller list September 22, 1974.

In this atmosphere of heated political debate, the conservative sociologist Helmut Schelsky published his notorious essay on Böll. Schelsky makes no secret of his dislike of Böll as a person and as a writer, and he wants to explore why "such a man is taken seriously in our current society" (Schelsky 1975, 393). Schelsky has no reservations about exploring a literary text outside his own field, sociology, since he can read like anyone else and has a developed literary taste; he prefers Arno Schmid to dreary social authors like Böll, Walser, and others. Although Schelsky does not have a background as a literary critic, it would be too easy to discard his essay as incompetent. His literary judgments may be highly questionable, but his approach deserves to be examined as a summary of conservative prejudices against Böll's political stance. Schelsky's main premise is embedded in the title of his essay, "Cardinal and Martyr" ("Kardinal und Märtyerer"; 1975). Schelsky claims that Böll wants to be the spiritual leader of a new political community in Germany, which is indeed correct, since Böll's last novels originated in ideas connected with the student movement of the 1960s and eventually led to the creation of a

[1] "Ich fordere die ganze Bevölkerung auf, sich von der Terrortätigkeit zu distanzieren, insbesondere auch den Dichter Heinrich Böll, der noch vor wenigen Monaten unter dem Pseudonym Katharina Blum ein Buch geschrieben hat, das eine Rechtfertigung von Gewalt darstellt."

new party, the Greens. Schelsky charges in a tongue-in-cheek argument that he first regarded Böll's whiny books "as unreal caricatures" of Böll's political ideas until he noticed that Böll was in fact too simpleminded to appreciate Schelsky's irony. Böll's constant complaining enraged Schelsky, since foreign readers of Böll's literature would get a wrong impression of the conditions in Germany. As a sociologist who is used to working with clearly defined hypotheses and theories, Schelsky cannot appreciate Böll's obscure way of thinking and his strangely unclear way of expressing himself. Böll's deficiencies are especially conspicuous in his anarchist relationship to violence, in which Schelsky perceives Böll as an advocate of terrorism. Schelsky understands very well that Böll's reasons for his aggressive or terrorist behavior toward German federal institutions originate in his experience of the Nazi terror machine; Böll considers the new German police and justice system a continuation of the Nazi system.

In reading Schelsky's book, it becomes increasingly clear that through Böll, Schelsky wants to knock down the entire German opposition, which he perceives as a huge conspiracy of liberal intellectuals. These intellectuals are busy replacing the established Christian religion and Western values with a new "social salvation philosophy" ("soziale Heilsgläubigkeit"; Schelsky 1975, 346), based on Marx's destructive materialistic ideas. According to Schelsky, that is the real reason why Böll is so interested in the Soviet writers' movement; he intends to use it as a model for his own movement in Germany; his connections with the Soviet Union are moves to increase his own power position in this new organization. The basis for Böll's dreams of power, according to Schelsky's thinking, is Böll's belief in an ultimately autonomous position for the writer within society. Schelsky calls this the "cardinal status" from which the writer can direct society, and since he is interested only in intellectual freedom for writers, as is manifest in his appeals for freedom directed only at imprisoned writers in the Soviet system, he has no interest in freedom for the masses (350). Schelsky recounts the quarrels surrounding the Meinhof article, viewing the North Rhine–Westphalian Interior Secretary Posser as the voice of reason against the unreasonable Böll, and he recounts Dolf Sternberger's attempts to expose Böll's thinking as a sham. For Schelsky, Posser and Sternberger represent and defend the social-political achievements of the Enlightenment in this "intellectual melodrama"; Böll, on the other hand, is a new social-religious obscurantist ("sozial-religiöser Dunkelmann"; Schelsky 1975, 353) who uses the restlessness of the student generation to establish his own position of power. Schelsky believes it is because Böll considers himself so much the leader of a new social movement that his public letters are always directed at major political leaders, the president or the commissioner of the police.

Although it seems here as if Schelsky tries to understand Böll, he in fact believes Böll is a seriously disturbed individual whose statements come from a deeply felt anxiety, and he regards him as a real enemy with real power. Schelsky concludes that he understands Böll's fixation on the Springer newspaper empire, since Böll is as interested as Springer in monopolizing public opinion (324). Schelsky's book ends with a condescending review of *The Lost Honor of Katharina Blum*, where all positive characters are either "of Jewish descent, or Communist, are either related to victims of anti fascism or other Nazi terror," and are elevated to a saintly status. Although it hardly seems necessary to discuss these allegations any further, this book gives a representative summary of the conservative attacks on Böll and clearly illustrates the racist bias of their arguments.

Hans Rudolf Müller-Schwefe continued some of Schelsky's arguments in his discussion of blasphemous elements in Böll's work (Müller-Schwefe 1978). Unlike Schelsky, Müller-Schwefe focuses on Böll as an author involved in a Christian crusade against "public evil" ("das öffentliche Böse"; Müller-Schwefe 1978, 154). This evil entered society after World War II, when the Germans had a chance to create a "good Christian" society on their soil as a succession to the previous evil government. However, remilitarization and the emergency laws (*Notstandsgesetze*) were two occasions on which evil entered once again into West German society. Thus parties, not just the CDU but also the SPD; the state and its institutions, especially the police; and finally the press, notably the *Bild Zeitung*, are carriers of this perceived evil (154). From this position, Müller-Schwefe understands Böll's work as an experimental counter-church in writing, which the critic condemns nonetheless as blasphemous. This experimental counter-church in Böll's writing is evident in the attempted portrayal of Leni as a worldly saint, when her sexual activities are seen as a sacrament, or when Boris's penis is described as the savior. All of this concludes with Müller-Schwefe's claim that Böll's literary activities are blasphemous. He predicts that Böll will in the end not succeed with his social plans, due to the artificiality of his supposed religion.

After Böll had finally won his much-publicized libel suit against the conservative TV-commentator Matthias Walden in 1982, the academic conservatives lost interest in Böll. In the late 1970s Böll was no longer as great a threat, since his writing had lost its edge, and the mood in the country became more congenial for the conservatives. For a final conservative voice, we should look at Ulsamer's book (Ulsamer 1987), which summarizes "more or less inadequately" (Balzer 1990, 52) what others (like Schelsky) had said before him. However, Ulsamer adds a few new ideas, for example a psychoanalytical explanation of Böll's need to write, developed from Alexander Mitscherlich's theory, that Germans had not yet fully comprehended the sorrows of the past ("Ein trauriges Land, aber ohne Trauer"; Ulsamer 1987, 29). However, Ulsamer does not approve of this tendency and calls all leftist writers "propagandists of misery" ("Elendspropagandisten"; Ulsamer 1987, 88). Ulsamer restates Schelsky's conspiracy theory, saying that Böll writes with the intention of becoming the priest of a new social religion and that he propagates an artificial misery that he would remove, once in power. Young people especially are attracted to that kind of "religious cult," and they will be ruined forever if Böll's activities are not stopped. Ulsamer attacks Böll along with the Gruppe 47 as the major force trying to overthrow the "Christian-Western traditions" ("christlich-abendländische Traditionen"; 255). He obviously overlooked the fact that by the time he published his book in 1987, Gruppe 47 had been defunct for fifteen years.

4. During the 1970s Böll was changing more and more from a writer of fiction to a political person. He soon became Germany's one-man moral and political opposition. As we have seen, traditional reviewers were slow to react, and it took a whole new generation of critics to understand his new attitude. Therefore, it was not until the mid-1970s that the whole picture of Böll's political involvement began to emerge in the public conscience, since both conservative *and* liberal critics refused to see the "complete, undivided Böll" ("den ganzen,

ungeteilten Böll"; Ziltener 1980, 2, 16). There was no complex literary system, although Böll tried to define his dialectical system as the "Aesthetics of the Humane" ("Ästhetik des Humanen") in the "Frankfurt Lectures." The "Lectures" contains Böll's beliefs that love for home (*Heimat*) and his own geographical region, memory, and language constitute the human being. The popular attitude in Germany of despising regionalism is countered by Böll with his argument that important works of art have been created in remote places such as Dublin (by James Joyce) or Prague (by Franz Kafka). Böll's literary position is "engaged"; the poet exists to analyze the "garbage of society" ("Abfall der Gesellschaft") and to take the place of a political opposition that – according to Böll – no longer existed in West Germany at that time. The Grand Coalition of the CDU and the SPD from 1965 to 1969 only confirmed Böll's political fears. The "Lectures" consists essentially of questions, the "search for a habitable language in a habitable country" ("die Suche nach einer bewohnbaren Sprache in einem bewohnbaren Land"; Böll 1978, vol. 2: 53).

Hanno Beth was the first to devote a collection of essays to political aspects of Böll's writing (Beth, *Einführung* 1975). Two of the essays have been discussed earlier in this volume, Stephen Smith's essay in the section on Anglo-American criticism (Smith 1975) and Peter Schütt's rejection of Raddatz's Marxist analysis of Böll's writing as a bourgeois maneuver (Schütt 1975). In one of his two essays in this volume, Beth comments on the quarrel between Raddatz and Schütt and seems to side somewhat with Peter Schütt's Marxist interpretation, from which he ridicules both Raddatz's and Gaus's social-democratic viewpoint. (Gaus's article had also appeared in Reich-Ranicki's volume.) Beth writes that both Raddatz and Gaus are disappointed that the political Böll does not go along with their own ideas (Beth 1975, 196). Using Habermas's theory concerning the role the press plays in changing our political patterns, outlined in Habermas's book *Strukturwandel der Öffentlichkeit*, Beth admires Böll's ability to uncover the "structural violence in the press," although he occasionally presents faulty details due to Böll's unfamiliarity with the operation of the press. In an attempt to balance Schütt's extremist "people's front" (*Volksfront*) ideology, Beth included Hermann Glaser, a more conservative writer. Glaser does not like Böll's political essays because they have no bite, there is "no ax that could break up our ice"

(Glaser 1975, 151). Böll does not have the intellectual caliber of a writer like Thomas Mann, and in comparison with Mann, Böll's prose looks like newspaper articles about petty problems, interesting one day and forgotten the next.

Beth ends his book with another essay by Jochen Vogt on the discussion of "The Balek Scales" similar to the one he had published in Reich-Ranicki's book (Vogt 1975). Vogt's insistence on this story, its potential for suggesting social change, and his emphasis on Cesare Cases's interpretation published in Reich-Ranicki's book contributed to the fact that this story eventually became an important focalizer for uncovering Böll's political potential in his writings. Vogt argues that the story is simple enough for teachers to use in their classes – in fact, partly due to Vogt's insistence, the story has since become one of the staple teaching tools in high schools, according to Sowinski. Students can relate to a twelve-year-old boy as the protagonist, and they can understand the social implications of law at this age (Sowinski 1988, 93). Vogt, who is a professor for the pedagogy of German literature, wanted to introduce the students to the idea of understanding social antagonisms through literature.

5. Jochen Vogt, along with Christian Linder and Heinrich Herlyn, has become one of the main leftist (or liberal) interpreters of Böll's political intentions. Vogt followed Batt's, Linder's, and Herlyn's explanations of the social upheaval of their time using Herbert Marcuse's theory of the "Great Refusal." Vogt's book is the most elaborate application of this theory, and offers a good introduction to the political atmosphere of the 1970s (Vogt 1978-1987). Vogt applies Böll's term *continuous writing* (*Fortschreibung*), but reminds the reader of Böll's dialectic method of which continuous writing is only one side, the other being *connection with tradition* (*Gebundenheit*). Vogt explains Böll's traditional writing style as a direct consequence of this dialectical moral concept, incorporating both connection with tradition and continuous writing. Vogt calls Böll's early style sacred realism ("sakraler Realismus"), in which he shows his Christian ideas in basic human (or existential) situations. Böll thereby creates in his stories a basic situation applicable to all humans, not just to the German conditions after the war. Böll's cryptic style in his short stories was the perfect answer for the war generation that had

endured the many horrible shocks of the war. After having survived in intense situations these survivors dismissed the big political picture as irrelevant for their own existence. Like most other interpreters, Vogt points to Böll's inability to recognize the petit bourgeoisie as a principal reservoir for the fascist movement. Böll does not see the petit bourgeoisie as a class; he can show them only as individual members of society. However, unlike any other Marxist interpreter, Vogt admires Böll's art of presenting the petit bourgeois, and he praises the Filskeit episode in *Adam, Where Art Thou?* because the terror is explained by "social-psychological conditions," for example by Filskeit's petit bourgeois authoritarian past, which conditioned him toward authoritarian behavior and unfulfilled dreams of power (Vogt 1987, 46). Böll pursued similar models in his later texts, for example in the idyllic Bietenhahn episode in *The Unguarded House* and in *The Irish Journal* episodes. In each book Böll presents a pattern of alienation, both limited and clear, a combination of "instrumental rationality and basic irrationality" (Vogt 1987, 64),[1] a model of realistic writing that puts Böll in the nineteenth-century tradition of Thomas Mann's *Buddenbrooks*. However, there is one fundamental difference between Mann's and Böll's literature; unlike Thomas Mann's novel, which shows the downfall of a family, Böll shows the prosperity and *rise* of a middle-class family in the Fähmels of *Billiards at Half-Past Nine*, through whose perspective we learn about German history from 1907 to 1958. Thus *Billiards* is the historical continuation of Thomas Mann's family in the Twentieth century. While in *Buddenbrooks* the family home served as a symbolic focus, Böll uses the abbey as a key symbol in *Billiards*, since his intention had been to write "sacred realism" (*sakraler Realismus*), a term that Dieter Kafitz had introduced to Böll scholarship (Kafitz 1976, 81).

To Vogt, Böll's early and middle periods, the periods that include the short stories, and the novels *Billiards at Half-Past Nine*, *The Clown*, and *End of a Mission*, are not as important as the later Böll. Thus Vogt centers his entire thesis of Böll as a writer around the two political novels *Group Portrait With Lady* and *The Lost Honor of Katharina Blum*, for which he has the highest praise. In that sense, Vogt is really repre-

---

[1] "So entstehen begrenzte, aber anschauliche Modelle der Entfremdung [mit einem] Ineinander von instrumenteller Rationalität und grundsätzlicher Irrationalität ... ."

sentative of the new generation, especially if compared to Schwarz, the Canadian critic who appreciated only the early Böll. Vogt interprets Leni's character along Kurt Batt's lines as a utopian "art and dream figure" ("Kunst- und Traumgestalt"). He maintains that Böll has to use archaic literary models for his utopian vision in *Group Portrait* since his customary realistic style could not be realized in late-capitalist society (Vogt 1987, 118). Böll had to abandon his realism, and it is obvious that Böll's Leni is a construct of pure fantasy and does not have a sociological basis in our society. Vogt obviously applies ideas that Kaiser had derived from his interpretation of German Classicism in his own review of *Group Portrait*.

Vogt explains that Böll became less interested in aesthetic-utopian constructs in his literature after he had gotten involved in the political arena. At this time he was more interested in how the press invades private life, as explained by Habermas's theories in *Strukturwandel der Öffentlichkeit*. Vogt understands Böll's career as a political writer from his experience of having his personal life invaded by the public and the police, which, as we have seen, culminated in the novel *The Lost Honor of Katharina Blum*. Vogt praises the intuitive realism of *Katharina Blum* in portraying the practices of the Springer press – the accuracy of Böll's portrayal was later supported by Wallraff's exposure of the practices of the *Bild-Zeitung* in *Der Aufmacher*. Vogt obviously does not share the reservations of many journalists to Böll's inaccurate portrayal of newspaper operations.

Vogt's book concludes with the thesis that Böll's work depended to a large extent on the principle of hope (Bloch's *Prinzip Hoffnung)*, the utopianism that dominated German literature in the 1970s. However, Vogt admits, Böll's artistic achievement, his special mode of realism, the "sacred realism," found few imitators, and he did not become a twentieth-century Balzac or Dickens. Böll's style was not considered innovative; he was no "writer for our century" (*Jahrhun-dertschriftsteller*); his importance was more in the area of developing a political culture in postwar Germany (168). Thus Böll's interest in political writing was very important since it had psychological impli-cations for every German reader, but these implications are much more difficult to assess than textual innovations.

6. Christian Linder merged Marcuse's resistance to the existing system of power and Ernst Bloch's utopianism with a psychoanalytical method that relates Böll's writing exclusively to Böll's early childhood experiences. Linder's book is a result of long personal conversations he had with the author (Linder 1978, 1986). Not surprisingly, Böll rejected the book afterwards. Linder claims Böll is still caught in the values of his childhood, intimacy and closeness, whereas he could never accept the "mature" values of objectivity and distance. The small childhood world of Böll's family remained the standard for the adult Böll in his perception of the modern impersonal world (Linder 1986, 23). According to Linder, it is easy to read Böll's work as his attempt to resist technology and modernity with simple childhood values. Linder's psychoanalytical approach puts Böll's life "on the couch," and Böll's readers can sympathize with his reservation about being taken apart in such a manner. By defending the values of his childhood, Linder continues, Böll also defends the social class of his parents, the petit bourgeoisie. The small and cozy atmosphere of his upbringing is indeed portrayed in his essay "In Defense of the Laundry Room" ("Zur Verteidigung der Waschküchen"), in which Böll describes the *Kleinbürgertum* of his childhood with the "sentiments and scents" of his youth. Böll recalls his childhood years as very happy ones, since his parents were broadminded and understanding. Böll's earliest ideas of society were formed in those years when his parents allowed him to play with the children of the workers in their neighborhood, something that the professors, attorneys, architects, and bank directors strictly forbade their children.

Linder's approach becomes problematic when he ventures from his psychological explanation into an explanation of Böll's texts. Linder maintains that Böll's writing is closely connected to his *Kleinbürgertum*, which explains the puzzling antagonism of a politically progressive intellectual with an old-fashioned and antiquated writing style (Linder 1986, 15). Linder is trying to explain Böll's "artistic handicap" as a consequence of his childhood, and although he is more forgiving toward Böll's class background than most Marxists, he ultimately rejects it just the same.

Linder's perception of the petit bourgeoisie and their political inadequacy during the Nazi period follows Karl Marx's view of this class. Marx believed that the petty bourgeois put a wedge into his dualistic perception of society, since this group did not know its place between the two antagonists, the bourgeoisie and the working class, and thus prevented the final revolution from happening.

> The petit bourgeois is like the historian Raumer, who is composed of 'on the one hand' and 'on the other hand'; in his economic interests and therefore in his political viewpoint, his religious and aesthetic views, in his morals, in everything. He is the antagonism itself. (Marx/Engels 1969-1975, vol. 16: 371)[1]

Although Marx's explanation was often attacked as inadequate, West Germany's neo-Marxists like Vogt, Linder, and later Herlyn used this explanation for their definition of the petit bourgeoisie.

7. Heinrich Herlyn endorses Marcuse's concept of the Great Refusal and distances himself from Linder's approach, using Bloch's utopia category "without reservation" (Herlyn 1979, 126). Marcuse had applied Freud's ideas of repression and finds his utopia in "the return of repressed childhood visions." Marcuse understands history as a mechanism of ever-increasing repression and alienation which needs to be reversed through a revolution, unlike Bloch's image of history as a "linear and automatic line of progress" toward "hope" (Herlyn 1978, 126). Herlyn argues that Böll's conservatism does indeed affect and modify his utopian intentions. Herlyn recognizes Freud's pleasure principle in Leni's character in *Group Portrait*, which, along with the reality principle, constitutes the dialectical tension of Böll's utopian thinking. Böll indirectly confirmed Herlyn's (and Vogt's) analysis in an interview:

> No, I really don't see myself as a dualist. Perhaps my philosophical, analytical, and systematic skills, and my diligence are not developed enough to work it out in any other form than novels or short stories . . . . (Ziltener 1980, 166)[2]

---

[1] "Der Kleinbürger ist wie der Geschichtsschreiber Raumer zusammengesetzt aus einerseits und andererseits. So in seinen ökonomischen Interessen, und daher in seiner Politik, seinen religiösen und künstlerischen Anschauungen. So in seiner Moral, so in everything. Er ist der lebendige Widerspruch."

[2] "Nein, ich empfinde mich wirklich nicht als Dualist. Wahrscheinlich ist meine philosophische, analytische und systematische Begabung oder auch mein Fleiß zu gering, um das anders als in Form von Romanen und Erzählungen darzustellen . . . ."

In taking the reader through *Group Portrait*, Herlyn admits to inconsistencies in Böll's narrative structure. A major weakness, according to Herlyn, is the wrong term Böll applies to Leni's class background, that of a proletarian, which reinforces his complete lack of understanding social classes. However, if Böll is not a sociologist, he still has a better intuitive understanding of the working-class mentality than most other writers and the students of the '68 generation, whose objectives the workers never grasped (Ziltener 1980, 69). With his book Herlyn captured a trend in German criticism of the 1970s which forgave a writer his weaknesses if he had the proper conscience. Herlyn later expanded his theory of the subversive character from Leni in *Group Portrait* to Katharina Blum, although Katharina was a successful modern woman and not a dropout from society. Herlyn claims that Katharina retains so many "subversive" characteristics, such as her erotic sensibility, that she could be Leni's younger sister (Herlyn 1982, 64).

In yet another essay Herlyn develops his theory further and brings it more in line with the principles that Böll himself had expressed in the "Frankfurt Lectures," expanding on the term *garbage* ("Abfälligkeit" or "Abfall"). Herlyn uses Böll's novel *And Never Said a Word* to demonstrate the duality of the public world, where the "good" people Käte and Fred are always poor; they are "garbage," which Böll uses as a positive term. By belonging to the dark side, they completely negate Marcuse's achievement principle ("Leistungsprinzip"), which claimed that in our current society the "libido was transformed [by] the genital supremacy to a forced sexuality" (Herlyn 1992, 128).[1] A rejection of Marcuse's achievement principle would mean a rejecting of current perceptions of sexuality as achievement-oriented. And thus, Herlyn states that Fred and Kate dream of an Eros without sexuality, of a combination of a supremacy-free ("herrschaftsfrei") area without the traditional genital supremacy (Herlyn 1992, 128).

8. Walter Warnach published an essay in 1978 in which he showed a completely different side of Böll's political engagement. Warnach portrays Böll as a German nationalist who in the early 1960s had,

---

[1] "... eine Transformation, eine Umwandlung der Libido von der unter das genitale Supremat gezwungenen Sexualität zu der Erotisierung der Gesamtpersönlichkeit."

together with the artist HAP Grieshaber and the aristocrat Werner von Trott zu Solz, founded the Christian-Socialist periodical *Labyrinth*. With his 1978 essay Walter Warnach intended to correct the conventional image of Böll as a subversive petit bourgeois who undermined German political culture (Warnach 1978). His essay shows a completely different Böll, a Böll who was actively working on ideas of German nationhood. Warnach reports how Böll had spoken out for German unification in *Labyrinth*, since he felt "amputated" by living in West Germany, just one part of Germany. For Böll, being a German was not identical with being "a citizen of the Federal Republic" (Ziltener 1980, 87). In an interview Böll had described his idea of conserving his post–World War II dreams in this idealized Germany:

> If I am conservative – and I tend to assume I am, not only as an author but also as a citizen of our time – then I probably want to conserve what more or less united all Germans in 1945 . . . . The liberation, the expectations of a new state, of a new community after the time endured really together . . . , and I conserve, if I may say so, the moment of liberation permanently in myself. I almost live from this, do you understand, my entire life, my family life, even as an author. (Herlyn 1982, 72)[1]

Warnach understands Böll's 1961 position as a search for a process in which Germans could rediscover their own identity. The German identity had been lost not just to the Nazis but also in a long process that lasted centuries (Warnach 1978, 4-5). Böll laments that Germany never had a revolution, since the concept of the modern Western nation is a result of a revolutionary process. As a consequence, Germany has had various irrational outbursts of violence and war since the Thirty Years' War, which has gotten the country deeper and deeper into its historical impasse. (The major obstacle, according to Böll, that prevented Germany from realizing its full political power was the presence of the Allied powers.) However, Böll sees a possibil-

---

[1] "Wenn ich konservativ bin, und ich neige dazu, das anzunehmen, nicht nur als Autor, auch als Zeitgenosse, dann möchte ich möglicherweise das konservieren, was 1945 alle Deutschen mehr oder weniger verbunden hat. . . . Die Befreiung, die Hoffnungen auf einen neuen Staat, auf ein neues Gemeinwesen nach der wirklich gemeinsam erlittenen Zeit . . ., und ich konserviere, wenn ich das so ausdrücken soll, in mir den Augenblick der Befreiung permanent. Ich lebe fast davon, verstehen Sie, mein ganzes Leben, mein Familienleben, auch als Autor."

ity of overcoming the existing absurd dichotomy of two political systems on German territory in the idea of the "cultural nation," since the idea of being German does not have to be linked to any of the existing political divisions of countries. Böll considers himself a German in a very broad sense and rejects West German statehood as inadequate. Since this became a popular concept among leftist intellectuals who refused loyalty to their country, Böll was again held responsible by the conservatives (Carstens, Dregger) for denying an entire generation of young people the opportunity to identify with their country.

In 1983 Jürgen Förster edited a collection of essays about Böll which summarized the ten-year discussion from 1972 until 1982 about his political activities (Förster 1983). In this volume Herbert Class traces Böll's political ideas to Heinrich Mann's writings, whose motto "never to work for one party alone, but according to the rules of human decency" Böll adopted as his own, a motto that Jürgen Habermas rephrased as the duty of any "citizen to take his affairs into his own hands" (Class 1983, 20). Ursula Kirchhoff summarizes Böll's idea of the "habitable language in a habitable country" ("die bewohnbare Sprache in einem bewohnbaren Land"; Böll 1978, vol. 2: 53) and recognizes the relevance of Böll's ideas in the fact that life and living are increasingly endangered due to the increasing tendency of the state to invade the privacy of its citizens, and in the fact that the environment is increasingly endangered by commercial exploitation (Kirchhoff 1983, 47). As a writer and as a citizen, Böll works against the destruction of our inner sanctuary, the self and the family, and against the destruction of the outer sanctuary, nature. In discussing Raddatz's rejection of Böll, Renate Kühn compares Böll with the nineteenth-century philosopher Ludwig Feuerbach, who had been dismissed by Marx as a lost bourgeois waverer: "Raddatz still hopes that Böll may some day reverse his position, and be regained for the revolutionary cause" (Kühn 1983, 78). However, Böll, unlike Feuerbach, is no philosopher; he needs concrete examples rather than philosophical abstractions (Kühn 1983, 80). Kühn captured well the Marxist distrust of writers who were too interested in stories and life rather than philosophical principles. Political revolutionaries do not need stories to contemplate different real-life possibilities; they need straightforward directions.

9. In analyzing the conflict-ridden decade of the 1970s, Anette Petersen concluded that the political debates surrounding the Meinhof article and *Katharina Blum* "cannot be seen as an academic debate among literary critics trying to reach a level of objectivity, but rather as a forum for a quarrel dominated by political motives" (Petersen 1980, 83).[1] However, even on the Left more critical voices appeared. Hanjo Kesting, for example, sided with conservatives who felt attacked by Böll: considering that Böll discussed a very delicate subject with his novel by directly attacking the *Bild Zeitung* in his foreword, his surprise at the reaction he had provoked seems naive (Kesting 1980, 87).[2]

In an interesting comment on his earlier theories, Vogt later distanced himself from the approach used by the East German Kurt Batt, as well as those by Linder and Herlyn, claiming that he had never intended to use Freud's or Marcuse's theories but had applied Max Weber's terminology to interpret Leni's type of social behavior (in *Group Portrait*). Vogt describes how he modified Weber's concept of value-rationality ("Wertrationalität"), a system of behavior patterns and interactions that are complete in themselves, that stand in (subversive) opposition to the purpose-rationality ("Zweckrationalität"), "which defines the majority of our actions as mere means to achieve a purpose lying outside of them" (Vogt 1989, 117). Vogt explained the differences between Weber's conservative and Marcuse's refusal-principle as a difference between their individual utopian concepts. By regressing to Weber's more conservative approach, Vogt asserts that Linder's and Herlyn's optimistic and utopian visions of the 1970s were possible only at this particular time immediately following the 1968 student revolts, what Vogt calls a time of

---

[1] "Die heftige Debatte kann also nicht als eine Auseinandersetzung zwischen um Objektivität bemühten Litarturkritikern verstanden werden, sondern ist zu sehen als Forum für einen in hohem Grad von politischen Motiven bestimmten Streit."

[2] "Wer, wie Böll in der *Katharina Blum* ein heikles Terrain betritt, ein realistisches Milieu entwirft, wirkliche Dinge mit Namen nennt, wer die Praktiken der Boulevardpresse aufzeigen und entlarven will und, schließlich, dies nicht nur ganz abstrakt, in phantasievoller Fiktion versucht, sondern – in einer Vorbemerkung – Ähnlichkeiten mit den Pratiken der BILD-Zeitung für 'unvermeidlich' erklärt, der muß sich Ablehnung, Widerspruch, Meinungsstreit gefallen lassen, ja er fordert sie geradewegs heraus."

revolutionary change ("Umbruchszeit"). From his later viewpoint Vogt calls the student revolts a "time of illusions," although he senses that Böll's political literature could be understood only when social changes were necessary, as they had been required in 1949 (Vogt 1991, 114). When Vogt called his earlier approach illusionary, he indicated that even socially based Böll research was reaching a new phase.

D: Böll Revisited

1. By the mid-1980s, more and more critics felt the time was ripe to reassess Böll's work and to decide whether his political and aesthetic demands still conformed with the changed social conditions. This job was facilitated by the first publication of Böll's collected works, a clear sign that he had now achieved canon status and had become a classic (*Klassiker*) in Germany. Bernd Balzer, a literature professor, gave one of the best basic introductions into Böll's work in the foreword to the collected works (Balzer 1977). Balzer admits that he is astonished by Böll's popularity; more than fifteen books, twenty dissertations, and about twelve hundred articles in newspapers and magazines (in 1977!) had already been published. (By 1993 the numbers are three times as high; now more than sixty books have been written about Böll.)

In summarizing Böll's views, Balzer uses Böll's phrase *anarchy and tenderness* ("Anarchie und Zärtlichkeit") to oppose the organized political system of order and violence. As a romantic visionary, Böll dreamed of a " 'society void of profit and classes,' where 'man should then not have to work beyond what he really needs for life,' a society based on the principles of the fisherman in 'Anecdote to Lower the Work Ethic' (Anekdote zur Senkung der Arbeitsmoral), a utopian vision that he considers realistic" (Balzer 1977, 116).[1] As Balzer's goal was to provide a solid introduction to Böll's work, its background, themes, and characters for a general reader, he was not interested in participating in the critical debate about whether Böll had a philo-

---

[1] "Eine 'profitlose und klassenlose Gesellschaft' schwebt ihm dagegen vor, in der 'der Mensch nicht arbeiten sollte über das hinaus, was er wirklich zum Leben braucht': eine Gesellschaft also, die nach der Philosophie des Fischers in der 'Anekdote zur Senkung der Arbeitsmoral' verfährt; eine Utopie, die er für 'romantisch, aber verwirklichbar' hält."

sophical system for his work. Balzer wrote several introductions to individual works as well as to the whole and has done perhaps more to popularize Böll's work than any other academic reviewer (Balzer 1981, 1990, 1992).

Since Marcel Reich-Ranicki had great influence on the Böll reception in the 1960s, it seems fitting to finish the Böll decade with a summary of his reviews that were published in book form between 1979 and 1986 (Reich-Ranicki 1979, 1986). These collections afford us a chronological study of the evaluations by Böll's most influential reviewer. Although strongly committed to excellence in style and form, Reich-Ranicki became the main admirer of Böll's moral involvement. He believed that many postwar German writers surpassed Böll in craftsmanship but that no postwar writer was loved like Böll, and "we only love those for whom we can feel sympathy" ("... vielleicht können wir nur lieben, wo wir auch etwas Mitleid empfinden"; Reich-Ranicki 1979, 100). Reich-Ranicki believed that Böll's artistic shortcomings worked to his advantage, as "imperfect" literature often does, since it did not overwhelm the reader but rather let him take part in the creative process. Böll's self-pitying attitude about his fame and the intrusion of the public into his privacy is met by Reich-Ranicki with ridicule about the author Heinrich Böll who does not seem to understand that he is one of the most powerful writers in Germany and Europe, who tremendously enjoys the role he plays for the media as "conscience of the nation" (Reich-Ranicki 1979, 119, 122). What remains is definitely Reich-Ranicki's admiration of Böll as a "moral authority" ("moralische Instanz"); he compared Böll with Thomas Mann in his function as ambassador or president of German literature. Even Böll's last bitter, sad book, *Women in a River Landscape*, reinforces Böll's role as the representative of Germany's moral conscience unlike any other writer in Germany.

Reich-Ranicki began his critical assessment of Böll's work with the belief that Böll had not written anything that could be considered perfect "except for a few short stories" (Reich-Ranicki 1963, 120). Reich-Ranicki recognized Böll's short-story style as his trademark and believed he should never have entered into novel writing. None of his novels can be compared with the quality of the short stories. He expressed his distinct discomfort with *The Clown* as a book written by a "malcontent." In another review, of *Absent Without Leave*, Reich-

Ranicki criticized Böll for copying fashionable styles; whereas he should keep the writing style that had been his trademark, he should keep writing the style that came naturally to him ("wie ihm der Schnabel gewachsen ist"; Reich-Ranicki, 1964; 1986, 54). And therefore he condemned *Absent Without Leave* along with *The Clown*:

> In Böll's *The Clown* was documented what later Grass had dominate *Local Anesthetic*: the literary and symbolic treatment of conflicts is replaced by direct grumbling about them. . . . With Hans Schnier, the grumbling clown, the social-critical engagement, which before had been a component of the story, itself becomes the hero of the story. (Reich-Ranicki 1973, 107)[1]

After Reich-Ranicki's negative reviews of *Group Portrait* (mentioned in chapter 4, section B, in this book), one would have expected an even stronger condemnation of *The Lost Honor of Katharina Blum*, but Reich-Ranicki praised the book as hitting "the German present right in the heart" (Reich-Ranicki 1974; 1986, 77),[2] since it showed Böll's strong moral commitment. Reich-Ranicki's praise may also be explained by the relatively short form of the novella, which Böll managed so well. Like most critics, Reich-Ranicki was quick to condemn *The Safety Net* (*Fürsorgliche Belagerung*) as weak and questionable, due to the "pathetic" style: "Who except Böll could afford to write so poorly in this country?" ("Wer außer Böll könnte es sich hierzulande leisten, so schlecht zu schreiben?"; Reich-Ranicki 1986, 102). Böll is no Grass, no Max Frisch, not even a Wolfgang Koeppen or Thomas Bernhard. There is not a single masterpiece among his works, with the exception of a couple of his early short stories.

Next to Reich-Ranicki's reviews for the *Frankfurter Allgemeine*, Joachim Kaiser's articles in the *Süddeutsche Zeitung* became the other important opinion maker for the reception of Böll's work in West Germany. Kaiser, who also wrote articles for scholarly journals, had given a detailed structural analysis of Böll's work and had supported

---

[1] "Bereits in Bölls *Ansichten eines Clowns* dokumentierte sich, was Grass später in *Örtlich betäubt* dominieren ließ: die Literarisierung und Symbolisierung der Konflikte machte einem direkten Räsonnement über sie Platz. . . . Mit Hans Schnier, dem räsonnierenden Clown, wurde das gesellschaftskritische Engagement, das zuvor der Erzählung immanent gewesen war, selbst zum ‚Helden' der Darstellung."

[2] ". . . die deutsche Gegenwart . . . mitten ins Herz . . . ."

Böll's aesthetic experiment in *Group Portrait*. Most of his reviews were reprinted in book form in 1988. As in his famous review article of *Group Portrait*, Kaiser's principle is apparently not to judge Böll's work from preconceived political ideas, but to develop his reading from the texts themselves, without subscribing to the author's perspective. Kaiser's precise procedure is unusual for a critic who normally does not reveal his criteria for evaluation. In his comparative method, both innertextual and intratextual, Kaiser discovers that *Frauen vor Fluß-landschaft* resembles *Billiards* in its ecstatic ("rauschhaft") structure, including the reader in its search for the ultimate truth. Kaiser does not condemn Böll's *Frauen vor Flußlandschaft* as easily as Reich-Ranicki did, since he admits to being confused and not having understood the author's concept; perhaps later we all might be able to recognize the book's importance (Kaiser 1988, 234). As Reich-Ranicki admired Böll's intense moral commitment, Kaiser marvels at Böll's sensitivity, which he reveals in his bottled-up tension (Kaiser 1988, 223).[1] For Kaiser, Böll is a Romantic genius.

Like Reich-Ranicki and Kaiser, Fritz Raddatz published his collected reviews in book form. When one surveys these essays, it becomes apparent that Raddatz (like Vogt and others) appears much more forgiving in his approach than he did in his earlier biting attacks; Raddatz also seems less interested in Böll, since he has realized that the older Böll would probably never change his attitude. However, Raddatz still asks with a sense of regret whether an "author of the rank and weight of Heinrich Böll would not have had the possibility of revolutionary practice" ("Hätte ein Autor von Rang und Gewicht des Heinrich Böll nicht doch die Möglichkeit der 'revolutionären Praxis'?"; Raddatz 1983, 151). Böll's biography appears to Raddatz to be a life of voluntary resignation. However, he credits Böll as being the best chronicler of West German life and society, "the Balzac of the second German republic" (Raddatz 1983, 153), a Marxist verdict that had been popularized by Georg Lukács. According to Friedrich Engels, Balzac was a novelist whose characters go beyond the limited perspective of the author:

---

[1] "Blickt man in diese von Böll gedichtete und von seiner Sensibilität geprägte Welt hinein, dann muß einem angst werden um Böll. Wie hält er das nur aus? Wie kann er weiterleben, wenn er mit solchen Spannungen fertig zu werden hat, wenn er geschlagen ist mit einer solchen Empfindsamkeit gegen die Münzen des Alltags?"

> That Balzac was therefore forced to act (in his books) against his own class interests and political prejudices, that he saw the necessity for a decline of his beloved aristocrats, and that he decided to draw them as people who do not deserve any better; and that he saw the people of the future where they could only be found at that time – that I consider as one of the greatest triumphs of realism, and as one of the greatest achievements of the old Balzac. (Marx/Engels 1969-1975, vol. 37: 44)[1]

According to Engels, Balzac's ideological backwardness is typical for bourgeois artists whose literature takes the progressive initiative over the artist himself in this dialectical process. Thus Raddatz considers Böll's literature far more progressive than the petit bourgeois Böll himself; literature can indeed achieve its own progress in this dialectical process. It seems that even the most radical of Böll's critics had come a long way to approve now of the once beleaguered artist, the surest sign that the battles were over and Böll was no longer dangerous.

   2. Heinz Ludwig Arnold updated his volume on Böll in the *text+kritik* series for the third time in 1982. Several of the articles in this collection of essays have been discussed elsewhere: Jochen Vogt's essay on short stories, Henry Glade's history of the reception in the Soviet Union, Heinrich Herlyn's discussion of Marcuse's refusal-principle, along with Klaus Schröter's and Arpád Bernáth's essays. The remaining four articles focus on the most common research topics of the 1980s:
   a. Heinz Hengst begins the current discussion of Böll's Catholicism in West Germany by concentrating on Catholicism as a subversive element in Böll's writing. According to Böll, religion should have nothing in common with the official church, as the "state church" is no longer "responsible for transcendental phenomena, for miracles, their very own area of expertise" (Hengst 1982, 113).[2] And therefore

---

[1] "Daß Balzac so gezwungen war, (in seinen Büchern) gegen seine eigenen Klassensympathien und politischen Vorurteile zu handeln, daß er die Notwendigkeit des Untergangs seiner geliebten Adligen sah und sie als Menschen schilderte, die kein besseres Schicksal verdienen; und daß er die wirklichen Menschen der Zukunft dort sah, wo sie damals allein zu finden waren – das betrachte ich als einen der größten Triumphe des Realismus und als einen der großartigsten Züge des alten Balzac."

the perceptive writer has to show the transcendental potential in religion. In this context Arpád Bernáth reviews Böll's first novel, *A Soldier's Legacy*, which was not published until 1982, as a novel that already includes Böll's theological program and should be interesting to both the casual reader and the Böll specialist (Bernáth 1982, 36).

b. Klaus-Michael Bogdal discusses Böll's merits as a school author following Jochen Vogt's arguments about Böll, who was abused by conservative school administrators. Bogdal gives an insightful introduction into the current situation in the school with his disheartening observation that ten years after Jochen Vogt's initial essay, the existentialist interpretations again dominate the school discussions of Böll's earlier short stories. The inability to give a proper interpretation of Böll's stories of the 1950s seems to reflect a widespread inability to deal with the German past in German school curricula. However, there are positive signs, since *The Lost Honor of Katharina Blum* has become the most popular Böll novel in school editions, and the "Anecdote to Lower the Work Ethic" has replaced "The Balek Scales" as Böll's most popular short story in anthologies (Bogdal 1982, 127).

c. Manfred Lange points to Bernd Balzer's and Joachim Kaiser's careful interpretations as an appropriate "new" method to read Böll's texts starting from their own structural potential. Lange appeals to the reader to "read" a text — not to impose an outside perception upon it, but rather "to immerse himself in the text with its conditions and perspectives, abandon any preconceptions, and adjust the method of interpretation to the text's own conditions" (Lange 1982, 92).[1] As mentioned earlier, similar literary methods had been used in the 1950s and 1960s in connection with Wolfgang Kayser's and Emil Staiger's approaches but were forgotten in the heat of the political debate of the 1970s.

d. Volker Neuhaus discusses the political dimension of Böll's novels for the 1980s by applying Habermas's ideas of the press invading privacy (*Strukturwandel der Öffentlichkeit*). Neuhaus dismisses the Marxist notion (Raddatz) that Böll is a chronicler of the Federal

[2] "Die Kirche und ihre Repräsentanten fühlen sich für übersinnliche Phänomene, für Wunder, ihren ureigensten Kompetenzbereich nicht mehr zuständig."

[1] ". . . sondern sich auf den Text in seinen Voraussetzungen und Perspektiven einzulassen, die eigenen Strukturen zur Disposition zu stellen, das Interpretationsinstrumentarium auf die Literatizität des Textes abzustimmen."

Republic, their "Balzac." Neuhaus also refers to Balzer's method of questioning the text itself and thereby uncovering Böll's use of satire for portraying society. Neuhaus reads most of Böll's later texts as satirical literature in order to uncover structural changes in comprehending reality; his method is similar to Friedrichsmeyer's approach (Neuhaus 1982, 38-41).

3. With so much attention on political issues, liberals focused their attention increasingly on the person Heinrich Böll, whose political interests they saw as corresponding to their own, as the essays by Peter Spycher, Ludwig Marcuse, and Jean Améry indicate (Ziltener 1980, 16). Everyone in the liberal camp wanted to claim Böll, the "left-liberal intellectual without party affiliation," for their own cause (Reich-Ranicki 1968). To meet this demand, the Böll family commissioned an "authorized" biography to affect somewhat the public image of Heinrich Böll. Christine Hoffmann, a trained journalist, is interested only in his life, not his books; she does not even consult his texts for his biography and limits herself to documents and interviews with friends and family (Hoffmann 1977–1986). Even in her criticism she never turns to opinions from the conservatives. The impression of this book is one of a nice present to the Böll family and to admirers of Heinrich Böll. Böll's brother Alfred wrote his own biographical account of their lives together (Alfred Böll 1981). And finally, a more critical biography came out as a Rowohlt monograph, written by the American Germanist Klaus Schröter (Schröter 1982). Like Linder, Schröter discusses Böll's family background as decisive in his perception of the world. Schröter cites several examples of contradictory scholarship about Böll which reflect the East-West tension in Germany, where it is impossible to write about a controversial author without alienating one side or the other.

4. It was not until 1976 that Dieter Kafitz introduced the term *sacred realism* (*sakraler Realismus*) to the Böll discussion; he had found that Böll's religious thinking did not allow a pure rationalistic, Enlightenment approach as Theodor Fontane and other nineteenth-century authors had, including Thomas Mann, but that his unique religious style found more and more imitators even in Germany (Kafitz 1976, 81). The Italian Germanist Maria dell'Agli was one of the

first to include a complete essay about religion in her introductory volume (dell'Agli 1984). The author of this article, Christoph Burgauner, writes that Böll's world should be understood from the Christian concept of grace (*Gnade*), which had been misunderstood when Böll used the term in the Meinhof debate. As a religious person, Böll would reduce the term to a legal meaning (as it is commonly used now); for him the Christian use of the word superseded all other uses. Burgauner argues that Böll's reading public did not follow his method of intentionally mixing religious meanings with secular ones, that it had been assumed that Böll would restrict his anarchistic ideals to his literary imagination (Burgauner 1984, 129).[1] However, Böll saw the social and religious world as one entity and believed the public would fault him if he did not apply the sensitivity of his fictional characters to people in the real world (Burgauner 1984, 129). Böll's actions were consistent with his thinking, where the reading public had wanted to divide him from his works. In his 1979 book *Jesus in der deutsch-sprachigen Gegenwartsliteratur* ("Jesus in German-speaking contemporary literature") Karl-Josef Kuschel focuses on the Negro spiritual in the title of *And Never Said a Word* which Böll relates to Käte's suffering. As the American blacks were able to express their suffering only through their songs, Kuschel maintains, Böll wrote about the human inability to communicate (*"Sprechen von der Unmöglichkeit zu sprechen"*; Kuschel 1979, 162). This inability according to Kuschel is the beginning of Böll's resistance to inhuman social conditions. In 1992 Kuschel expanded his theory of Böll's literary work as a "theology and anthropology of the sacramental" ("Theologie und Anthropologie des Sakramentalen"; Kuschel 1992, 163). He uses for his interpretation Böll's radio-play "Hausfriedensbruch" ("Trespassing") which he considers essential for the understanding of Böll's theology concept. Kuschel sees Böll's oeuvre as an attempt to show universal religious problems from an individual perspective, for example, from the perspective of the "little people" (Kuschel 1992, 175).[2]

---

[1] "Das Publikum, gewöhnt an den leisen Ton von Trauer in Bölls Fernsehinterviews, hatte angenommen, daß sein anarchisch-idealistischer Radikalismus auf Gestalten der Imagination beschränkt bleiben werde, während Böll genau umgekehrt davon ausgehen mußte, daß ihm Charakterlosigkeit vorzuwerfen wäre, wenn er das Verständnis, das er für die verzweifelte Aggressivität erfundener Gestalten aufbringe, nicht auch für wirkliche Menschen beweise."

Manfred Nielen discusses Böll's religiousness in his texts and rejects Durzak's notion that Böll's secularized salvation models are idyllic and unrealistic. For Nielen, Böll's belief in the "pious family" provides an inner sanctity that helps man understand his own problems better. Nielen takes up Konrad Kurz's suggestion to regard Böll as "the great simplifier," as a teacher who constructs in his literature a (simplistic) model that enables people to understand better their own situations (Nielen 1987, 92). Nielen focuses on the "holy" family in *And Never Said a Word* and *Group Portrait*. Fred Bogner (of *And Never Said a Word*) finds the inner peace to solve his problems by watching the family in the snack shop – they help him discover the importance of the family as the essential church community. In order to understand his own problems and be united with their fundamental needs, Fred (along with others) needs to be isolated from the corrupt forces of society in order to find his way back to his family. In the same way, Leni contains charismatic elements which she uses to set up a refuge for social outcasts. All of these disciples or saint figures are represented by women, whom Böll viewed as morally superior to men.

In their co-authored book the radical-democratic literature professor Walter Jens and the Catholic theologian Hans Küng, both from Tübingen, came to similar conclusions about Böll's religion. Jens, the more cogent writer of the two, states that Böll's theology means to him that the more gentle and tolerant a human being is, the closer he is to the messianic center (Jens/Küng 1989, 71).[1] Jens combines Böll's Christian thinking with the ideas of Dostoyevsky, who had also tried to invoke Jesus as "our brother in everyday life" (77). And Küng adds that Böll did not depict an anachronistic Catholic world in his work; "no, his work manifests the common problems of every man!" (302); Böll is a "truly ecumenical figure" (313). These statements coming from a former radical socialist still seem unusual and are proof that even radicals have come back to understanding Böll in a manner that

---

[2] "Bölls Werk ist ein einziger großer Versuch, die universalen Probleme in partikularer Perspektive zu spiegeln, große Fragen aus dem Blickwinkel der kleinen Leute zu humanisieren."

[1] "Das ist, in nuce, Heinrich Bölls literarische Theologie: Je behutsamer, sanftmütiger, geduldiger, erbarmensfähiger ein Mensch sich verhält, lautet die These, desto näher steht er dem jesuanischen Zentrum."

would have been unimaginable a few years before; in the 1960s, the only possible salvation had to be Enlightenment-based as outlined by Marcuse and Bloch.

5. Under the changed social conditions in the late 1980s, a new interest in reappraising Böll's entire work along Balzer's lines emerged, rejecting Marxist interpretations as limited and searching for meaning in the text alone. As the interest in Böll's last two best-sellers, *Group Portrait With Lady* and *The Lost Honor of Katharina Blum*, was fading, his earlier books received more attention. In a recent interpretation of *And Never Said a Word*, Ernst Ribbat states that German studies often misinterpreted Böll and owe Böll's works new interpretations (Ribbat 1981, 53; dell'Agli 1984, 39).[1] Ribbat alludes to Böll's insistence on the autonomy of the author; if Böll insists so stubbornly on the special status of his literature we should take him at his word. Klaus Jeziorkowski, who was one of the first existentialist interpreters of Böll's work (Jeziorkowski 1968) and whose method seemed outdated, celebrates a comeback after twenty-five years (Jeziorkowski 1983). He confirms the observation of a "renaissance of existentialism after the end of the neo-Marxist rebellion," which according to Jeziorkowski is indicated by "a paradigm change from Adorno to Heidegger, from Brecht to Hölderlin" (Jeziorkowski 1983, 273). Jeziorkowski just has to go back to his own existential paradigms, and once again he calls *Adam, Where Art Thou?* a basic document of German postwar existentialism. Böll presents an archetypal situation, the first two men after they have eaten from the fruit of knowledge, and the continuation of a dualistic structure – similar to Schnitzler's *Reigen* – shows the total absurdity of war as a medieval dance of death (Jeziorkowski 1983, 281).

Jeziorkowski shows his knowledge of modern interpretation techniques and introduces Paul deMan's deconstructionist methods to Germany, trying to close the gap between the more advanced Western European methods and Germany's social methods. Jeziorkowski bases his interpretation of Böll on deMan's "allegory of reading" and interprets Böll's texts as "complex signs" ("Zeichenensembles";

---

[1] "Die Germanistik nämlich, diese Voraussetzung sei gemacht, ist auch Bölls Werken Interpretationen schuldig."

Jeziorkowski 1992, 161). In fact, Jeziorkowski's method of analysis turns out to be a skillful combination of methods from other art forms, for example, the visual arts and music theory. In *Adam, Where Art Thou?* Jeziorkowski observes a "spatializing" of time ("Verräumlichung der Zeit"; Jeziorkowski 1992, 140), which he considers a key element in modern narration techniques, found in most modern texts by Proust, Joyce, Virginia Woolf, and Thomas Mann. According to Jeziorkowski, this spatializing culminates in *Adam, Where Art Thou?* in the medieval dance-of-death icon which combines the novel's independent scenes with the experience of death. As the plague had been the cause for mass deaths in medieval times, war is regarded by Böll as the cause for death; war is a disease, as Böll had pointed out in his motto based on Antoine de Saint-Exupéry's thoughts. In his later novels, however, Böll changed his structural pattern: *Billiards at Half-Past Nine* reminded Jeziorkowski of the abstract paintings of Piet Mondrian, Paul Klee, and Joan Miró which he sees as spatial embodiments of the pool game. And consequently, Jeziorkowski concluded that Böll's final novel, *Women in a River Landscape*, is a deliberate "association with the arrangements of paintings and photographs" ("Assoziation mit den Arrangements von Gemälden und Fotografien"; Jeziorkowski 1992, 158). Jeziorkowski seems to have found an adequate interpretation to this novel with his deconstructionist method. While Jeziorkowski's structural analysis convinces, it still falls short when he explores Böll's philosophical foundation and when he claims that all of his work shares a similar "existential basic sorrow" ("existentielle 'Grundtrauer'"; Jeziorkowski 192, 161) – the critic apparently has not changed his philosophical position much from his earlier interpretations. A similar interpretation of Werner Janssen fails when he tries to find "the eternal return of wholeness" ("Stetige Wiederkehr einer Ganzheit") in Böll's work (Janssen 1984, 207). As these two examples show, German post-structuralists use worthwhile interpretation methods in their structural approaches, but have a problem combining their discoveries with the philosophical underpinnings – terms like "existential sorrow" and "eternal wholeness" are too vague for their precise investigations.

By the 1980s, Böll's novel *The Clown* was his most popular. In a study on the relationship between reader behavior and the author, Martin Krumbholz shows how Böll, as an open-minded author, does not guide his reader in a restrictive manner. Since Schnier and Böll are not identical, it is up to the emancipated reader "to take the time to fill those open slots with his own norms" (Krumbholz 1980, 86).[1] Due to these open slots, Krumbholz argues that Böll did not produce a political pamphlet, but a sophisticated literary text. Karl Heinz Götze maintains it was partly Böll's faulty, inconsistent style that caused so many readers to confuse the author's opinion with that of the protagonist (Götze 1985, 166). However, Götze's book was the first straightforward praise of Böll's novel, and he credits the unique blend of Catholicism, repressed (Nazi) past, and "the money-fetish" for the persistent popularity of The Clown in Germany. In his thorough explication of its popularity, Götze shows that the discussion of The Clown centered around church criticism and Böll's concept of sex as a sacrament; however, the implied critique of capitalism was completely overlooked. According to Götze, the novel is Böll's attempt to offer complete criticism of Adenauer's conservative government at a time when no one, not even the opposing Social Democrats, could offer a viable political alternative. Götze's new, more complex, interpretation of The Clown explains the renewed attention this novel was getting in the 1980s as a text embodying many of the lost ideals of the Marxist student revolts. Götze, whose ideas are obviously indebted to the 1960s generation, hoped to rekindle a revolutionary spark in the stagnant neoconservative mood of the 1980s with his interpretation of The Clown. One of Bernd Balzer's books of interpretation discusses The Clown and includes extensive documentation about the book's reception in 1963. Balzer discusses feminism (he cites Beck's ideas), as well as Böll's perception of the saintly woman; this part is also well documented.

Since Böll's most political books, Group Portrait and The Lost Honor of Katharina Blum, had been claimed by the political Left for their cause in the 1970s, a change toward a more conservative approach was due here as well. In 1982 Hans Kügler attempted an interpretation for schoolteachers of Group Portrait in which he denies Marxists any

---

[1] "Also wurde in der Analyse eines Textausschnittes nach Leerstellen Ausschau gehalten, die Leserwertungen offenhalten (sie nicht restriktiv steuern). Das Ergebnis hat gezeigt, daß solche Leerstellen – ob nun intendierte oder "automatische" – in der Tat vorhanden sind; der reale Leser muß sich also das Recht nehmen, sie mit seinen eigenen Normen aufzufüllen."

access to this novel, since they, like Bernhard, operated from ready-made historic models instead of their own authentic experiences of time (Kügler 1982, 426).[1] He focuses on the author's personal experience as a starting point for interpretation, something that should be called a neopositivistic approach. Kügler rejects Bernhard's simplistic dichotomies of "exploiter versus exploited" ("Ausbeuter/ Ausgebeutete") and "property versus lack of property" ("Besitz/ Besitzlosigkeit") as ineffective teaching tools, since they simply represent clichés that are useless for understanding history (Kügler 1982, 482). Thus Kügler rejects the presumption of a reception-oriented (reader-text-oriented) theory of the text and claims that only a true didactic method focusing on the author "can uncover the special kind of a text as being historical and its relation to 'general history' " (Kügler 1982, 428).[2]

Edgar Bracht was the first to interpret the image of the Russian prisoner of war in *Group Portrait*. Bracht points to the striking *German* elements in the education of Boris Koltowski (the POW, Leni's lover). Unlike typical Russians at that time, he does not know much about his own culture, especially the proletarian literature of the 1930s – instead, his interests center on German early-twentieth-century literature from Trakl to Kafka (Bracht 1988, 95). Bracht concludes that Böll had political intentions in describing Boris's education, since Scholsdorff, the German in Böll's novel, is an avid reader of Russian literature; Böll was obviously trying to give an example of cooperation between the nations at a time when Brandt's *Ostpolitik* was getting started.

Even the political battle surrounding the novella *The Lost Honor* seemed to fade during the 1980s. When Schlöndorff's movie *The Lost Honor of Katharina Blum* was first shown in Germany, the director had to defend his (and Böll's) concept of violence when he was asked why the audience applauded Tötges's killing. Schlöndorff defended himself by describing the reaction as a plebiscite ("Volksabstim-

---

[1] " . . . daß das wirkliche, das Verhalten der Menschen bestimmenden Geschichtsbewußtsein sich nicht auf der Ebene der ideologischen und wissenschaftlichen Dikusssion bildet, sondern aus der skizzierten authentischen Zeiterfahrung unmittelbar hervorgeht."

[2] " . . . kann daher die besondere Weise der Geschichtlichkeit der Literatur und ihr Verhältnis zur 'allgemeinen Geschichte' . . . erschließen."

mung"), which determined the success of the film (Viktor Böll 1983). Therefore the success of this film depended largely on the fact that it directly represented the sentiments of the people. After seeing the film, Heidemarie Fischer-Kesselmann applied Kaiser's perspective to the movie as well and found Böll's unrealistic feminine ideas formulated in Immanuel Kant's writings. In comparing Katharina Blum with Kant's "aesthetic and moral ideal of a woman," Fischer-Kesselmann concludes that Kant saw women as "unhistorical," as "anthropologically" superior to men, as expressed in Kant's "natural basic law" (Fischer-Kesselmann 1984, 197).[1] This interesting source thus traces Böll's "angelic" women to a traditional German notion of the "pure" woman. The destruction of public life through the press is for Fischer-Kesselmann a "deprivation of bourgeois society" ("die historische Depravation der bürgerlichen Gesellschaft"), of eighteenth-century idealism and the rational economy of the capitalist society conflict in this novel (199). Her conclusion, completely in line with the social theories of the 1970s, turns out to be useless in its broad scope, since it is not backed up by textual evidence. Like Irene Compton, Dorothee Römhild investigates the origin of Böll's belief in women as the "saviors," and concludes that Böll believes the female character is predestined to save humanity – women are the model-citizens (Römhild 1991). Römhild criticizes Böll's concept as "distorted" ("verzerrt") and as inappropriate for social-critical literature (Römhild 1991, 214).[2]

Eberhard Scheiffele argues along Erhard Friedrichsmeyer's lines in regarding *The Lost Honor of Katharina Blum* as a satire and concludes that Böll had to resort to satire in a heated political atmosphere in which an innocent citizen is driven to murder. The basic premises of satire are fulfilled, according to Scheiffele; a distorted exaggeration of a dismal situation is presented. Therefore, Böll uses deliberately awkward language "to force the reader almost automatically to a language analysis, to language critic" ("daß der Leser buchstäblich von selbst

---

[1] "Sie versinnbildlicht ein ästhetisch-sittliches Frauenideal, wie es z. B. Kant als unhistorische, anthropologisch-natürliche Grundgesetzlichkeit beschrieben hat."

[2] ". . . die Frau ais letzer 'Hort' von Menschlichkeit - damit konstruiert Böll ein Bild, das gerade in gesellschaftskritischer Literatur so nicht haltbar ist."

zur Sprachanalyse kommt, zur Sprachkritik gedrängt wird"; Scheiffele 1984, 79).

6. The many articles, essays, and obituaries upon Heinrich Böll's death reflected his widespread popularity. The strongest praise was for Böll's moral stance and his importance for Germany's political development (Enzensberger, in Jens 1985; Höllerer 1986); Reich-Ranicki called him "Germany's moral teacher ("Praeceptor Germaniae"; Reich-Ranicki 18 Jul. 1985). Even Fritz Raddatz admitted that Böll was *the* political authority of the 1970s, while Bernhard criticized the conservatives who had once raged against "Böllshevism" and yet were ready to integrate him into their society at the end of his life (Raddatz 1985; Bernhard 1985).

However, even at Böll's death critical voices did not stop. Some critics still faulted Böll for his sloppy writing, for example Rudolf Augstein, who did not count Böll among the great writers of this century (Jens 1985; Augstein, in Jens 1985). Like most other critics, the Marxist Raddatz and the conservative Baumgart agreed on the failure of Böll's last novel, *Women in a River Landscape*. Their verdict points out that Böll had failed on two accounts: moral integrity, which had always been his strongest point; and narrative technique. Raddatz points to Böll's loss of physical energy reflected in this novel and believes that at the end of his life Böll's moral impetus had left him and he did not even care "to scream out loud"[1]; Raddatz adds that the novel reads like the work of a "dilettante" (Raddatz 1985). Conservatives such as the *Welt*-critic Günter Zehm are appalled at the extent of "artistic incompetence and stylistic indifference" (Zehm 1985),[2] while Baumgart wonders where in this novel art ends and kitsch begins. Baumgart still remembers Böll as the greatest German writer about the World War II experience that "represents a traumatic shock released in slow picture sequences that seem to explode out from a deep sleep" (Baumgart 1986, 557).[3]

---

[1] "Es lohnt ihm nicht einmal mehr, aufzuschreien . . . ."

[2] ". . . Ausmaß an künstlerischer Ohnmacht und stilistischer Gleichgültigkeit . . . ."

[3] ". . . die immer neu versuchte Durcharbeitung eines traumatisch erstarrten und grellen Schocks, der sich nun löst in stillen, langsamen, wie aus dem Tiefschlaf explodierenden Bildsequenzen."

Like Baumgart, Jeziorkowski summarized Böll's achievements at the end of his life. Jeziorkowski is now ready to integrate Böll's moral intentions into his analysis and recognizes his literature as theologically motivated. Böll's language, however awkward it may sound, is an honest attempt to reclaim language for humanism against the language abuse of officials like those at German immigration offices, who have constructed a "verbal Auschwitz" (Jeziorkowski 1988, 52). Jeziorkowski shows his admiration for Böll's ability to make us feel at home in his fiction; Böll does not simply provide a "continuum of space, but also of time"; his literature is "home literature" (Heimatliteratur) in the truest sense (Rademacher 1989, 63).

Frank Schirrmacher deliberately and polemically misrepresented Böll's intentions when he charged that with German unification the old West German literature as we had known it was finished (Schirrmacher 1990). With the focus of his attack obviously on Böll, the prototype of West German literature and its "type of civilization" ("der westdeutsche Zivilisationstyp"), Schirrmacher intentionally credits Böll with much more than he deserved, with masterminding the German liberal conscience that had developed over the previous twenty-five years. These arguments attacking Böll as stale and out of touch seem like Schelsky's recycled ideas. Jochen Vogt refuted Schirrmacher's claim by stating that Böll's premise for writing originated in his experience of National Socialism, which younger people such as Schirrmacher lacked (Vogt 1991, 9). Although the Nazis ruled for only twelve years, their existence influenced Germany far more seriously than the forty years of peace ever could. Böll had been directly affected by the Nazis (unlike the younger Schirrmacher); his redefinition of German nationhood would necessarily have to consider the Nazi past. As a participant in the war and eyewitness of Nazi atrocities Böll would continually warn against renewed Nazi activities or against conservatives who often did not even realize the degree to which they had been influenced by Nazi ideas.

7. As more and more heretofore unpublished material of Böll's work is finally appearing in print and a critical edition is being prepared (Der Spiegel 32: 1992, 150-51), a new and modified picture of the writer will emerge. In 1992 Balzer edited a collection of essays honoring Böll's seventy-fifth birthday which would have been on

December 21, 1992 (Balzer 1992). Balzer compared his own 1977/78 edition of Böll's work with the situation the Wuppertal working group under Werner Bellmann is faced with for the new edition. In 1977 Böll's archives were still located in Boston, virtually inaccessible to scholars from Germany. Therefore, the 1990s promise to become an important decade of German Böll research with the inclusion of most of Böll's unpublished work, for example, the diaries, of which only a selection has been published so far.[1]

The contributors in Balzer's volume outline the scope of coming research. Heinrich Vormweg investigates Böll's early unpublished work; Karl Heiner Busse investigates the political opinions of the early Böll and concludes that he differed vastly from the more nationalist writers in the periodical *Der Ruf*, the core of *Gruppe 47*. Vormweg writes that Böll had been critical of Catholic church policies since his early teenage years, and Busse adds that Böll's impressive independence was in the end the reason for his later enormous popularity and effectiveness (Busse 1992, 39). Balzer is mainly interested in reevaluating Böll as a writer of considerable aesthetic dimensions, something that had been largely ignored in Germany on account of his political impact. Balzer claims that Böll had been misread as a realistic author, and he cites the popular West German TV program *Titel - Thesen - Temperamente* that stated that Böll wrote with his fiction "one chapter after another of the post-Hitler-time. The summation of his stories has over the years become our own history" (*Titel - Thesen - Temperamente* 20 Oct. 1972; in Balzer 1992, 92).[2] On the contrary, Balzer claims, Böll was never primarily interested in "reality," but as a true artist began to work first with language — he developed the plot for *The Clown* from the word *labyrinth*, the title of the political journal to which he had been contributing. Therefore, Böll had always claimed that the war and reconstruction scenes were facades to his basic stories which could have been written in any time; political "reality" meant little to him. By including Jeziorkowski's and Friedrichsmeyer's structural interpretations in his volume, Balzer wants to emphasize

---

[1] Heinrich Böll. *Rom auf den ersten Blick*. Bornhein-Merten: Lamuv, 1987.

[2] "Mit jeder seiner Erzählungen hat er uns ein Kapitel der Nach-Hitler-Zeit nach dem anderen aufgeschrieben. Aus der Summe seiner Geschichten ist über die Jahre unsere Geschichte geworden."

more aesthetically oriented aspects in German Böll scholarship (Jeziorkowski 1992, Friedrichsmeyer 1992).

Likewise, Georg Guntermann reassesses Böll's popular "success" in West Germany during the high times as shallow and essentially misdirected, since his work had been misread as part of German common history ("wirkungsloser Erfolgsautor"; Guntermann 1992, 223). Guntermann sees on the one hand the public's expectations of utopian visions from Böll, beginning with the publication of his *Group Portrait With Lady*, whereas on the other hand Böll's own utopian visions were "regressive" (Guntermann 1992, 203). Guntermann regards Böll's political vision as synonymous with the old cardigan sweater his fictitious character, the auth. in *Group Portrait*, wears, and which he did not want to throw away. Increasingly, Böll realized he had to remain true to his upbringing as his identity, whereas West German society moved away from him (Guntermann 1992, 209).[1]

Böll's idea of neighborhood became indeed an important paradigm of Böll's utopian vision of a cooperative society. Böll captured with his own limited life in Cologne an experience that proved vital for the reconstruction of a modest West German sense of nationality. There were favorable circumstances, since although Böll was a regional writer for the lower Rhineland, he was also living and writing in an important intellectual and cultural center of West German political power during the Adenauer years, Cologne. His ability to maintain his roots, his religion, and his idealism during his political involvement proved to be his most important contribution to West German culture. Böll managed to give West Germans a sense of home in this world with his modest redefinition of the homeland ("Heimat") as the small place where engagement really makes a difference.

Böll's importance could not have been demonstrated in a clearer way than by Frank Schirrmacher's essay, in which he regards Böll as the most important writer for the shaping of West Germany's conscience (Schirrmacher 1990). As Schirrmacher's accusations show, a fin de siècle atmosphere is taking hold of Germany's new intellectual leadership, where the new generation, people like

---

[1] "Das 'Beharren des 'Verf.' auf seiner alten, vielfach gestopften Jacke' ist Inbegriff des Beharrens auf der behaupteten 'Mentalität des Alltäglichen' in der Literatur . . . ."

Schirrmacher, are beginning to evaluate the progress of the "old" Federal Republic in the last forty years. They regard his influence to be as great as that of politicians such as Konrad Adenauer or Willy Brandt. Just as we are beginning to reexamine the values of the old Federal Republic, so too Böll's work will have to be reexamined. Paradoxically, Böll will now be considered an "established" player in the shaping of the liberal political consciousness of the second German republic. And once again, political methods will most likely serve this purpose better than a purely literary or text-centered method, since his texts are concerned primarily with political ideas.

IV: BIBLIOGRAPHY

A. Primary Sources

Böll, Heinrich. 1949. *Der Zug war pünktlich: Erzählung.* Opladen: Middelhauve.

————. 1950. *Wanderer, kommst du nach Spa . . .: Erzählungen.* Opladen: Middelhauve.

————. 1951. *Die schwarzen Schafe: Erzählung.* Opladen: Middelhauve.

————. 1951. *Wo warst du, Adam? Roman.* Opladen: Middelhauve.

————. 1952. *Nicht nur zur Weihnachtszeit: Eine humoristische Erzählung.* Frankfurt: Frankfurter Verlagsanstalt.

————. 1953. *Und sagte kein einziges Wort: Roman.* Cologne: Kiepenheuer & Witsch.

————. 1954. *Haus ohne Hüter: Roman.* Cologne: Kiepenheuer & Witsch.

————. 1955. *Das Brot der frühen Jahre: Erzählung.* Cologne: Kiepenheuer & Witsch.

————. 1957. *Die Spurlosen: Hörspiel.* Hamburg: Hans-Bredow-Institut.

————. 1957. *Im Tal der donnernden Hufe: Erzählung.* Wiesbaden: Insel.

————. 1957. *Irisches Tagebuch.* Cologne: Kiepenheuer & Witsch.

————. 1958. *Doktor Murkes gesammeltes Schweigen und andere Satiren.* Cologne: Kiepenheuer & Witsch.

————. 1958. *Erzählungen.* Opladen: Middelhauve.

————. 1959. *Billard um halb zehn: Roman.* Cologne: Kiepenheuer & Witsch.

————. 1961. *Brief an einen jungen Katholiken.* Cologne: Kiepenheuer & Witsch.

————. 1961. *Erzählungen, Hörspiele, Aufsätze.* Cologne: Kiepenheuer & Witsch.

————. 1962. *Ein Schluck Erde: Drama.* Cologne: Kiepenheuer & Witsch.

———. 1963. *Ansichten eines Clowns: Roman.* Cologne: Kiepenheuer & Witsch.

———. 1964. *Entfernung von der Truppe: Erzählung.* Cologne: Kiepenheuer & Witsch.

———. 1966. *Die Spurlosen: Drei Hörspiele.* Leipzig: Insel.

———. 1966. *Ende einer Dienstfahrt: Erzählung.* Cologne: Kiepenheuer & Witsch.

———. 1966. *Frankfurter Vorlesungen.* Cologne: Kiepenheuer & Witsch.

———. 1967. *Aufsätze, Kritiken, Reden.* Cologne: Kiepenheuer & Witsch.

———. 1969. *Hausfriedensbruch: Hörspiel, Aussatz: Schauspiel.* Cologne: Kiepenheuer & Witsch.

———. 1971. *Gruppenbild mit Dame: Roman.* Cologne: Kiepenheuer & Witsch.

———. 1972. *Gedichte.* Berlin: Literarisches Colloquium.

———. 1973. *Neue politische und literarische Schriften.* Cologne: Kiepenheuer & Witsch.

———. 1973. *Versuch über die Vernunft der Poesie. Nobelvorlesung.* Stockholm: Norstedt & Söner.

———. 1974. *Die verlorene Ehre der Katharina Blum oder: Wie Gewalt entstehen und wohin sie führen kann: Erzählung.* Cologne: Kiepenheuer & Witsch.

———. 1975. *Berichte zur Gesinnungslage der Nation.* Cologne: Kiepenheuer & Witsch.

———. 1975. *Drei Tage im März: Ein Gespräch mit Heinrich Böll/Christian Linder.* Cologne: Kiepenheuer & Witsch.

———. 1975. *Gedichte: Mit Collagen von Klaus Staeck.* Cologne: Labbe und Muta.

———. 1977. *Einmischung erwünscht: Schriften zur Zeit.* Cologne: Kiepenheuer & Witsch.

———. 1977. *Werke: Romane und Erzählungen vol. 1: 1947–1951, vol 2: 1951–1954, vol. 3: 1954–1959, vol. 4: 1961–1970, vol. 5: 1971–1977.* ed. by Bernd Balzer. Cologne: Middelhauve/ Kiepenheuer & Witsch.

———. 1978. *Hörspiele, Theaterstücke, Drehbücher, Gedichte vol 1: 1952–1978.* ed. by B. Balzer. Cologne: Kiepenheuer & Witsch.

———. 1978. *Mein Lesebuch.* Frankfurt: Fischer.

————. 1978. *Werke: Essayistische Schriften und Reden vol 1: 1952–1963, vol 2: 1964–1972, vol 3: 1973–1978; Interviews vol 1: 1961–1978.* ed. by Bernd Balzer. Cologne: Kiepenheuer & Witsch.

————. 1979. *Du führst zu oft nach Heidelberg und andere Erzählungen.* Bornheim-Merten: Lamuv.

————. 1979. *Eine deutsche Erinnerung: Interview mit René Wintzen.* Cologne: Kiepenheuer & Witsch.

————. 1979. *Fürsorgliche Belagerung: Roman.* Cologne: Kiepenheuer & Witsch.

————. 1980. *Ein Tag wie sonst: Hörspiele.* Munich: Deutscher Taschenbuch Verlag.

————. 1981. *Was soll aus dem Jungen bloß werden? Oder: Irgendwas mit Büchern.* Bornheim-Merten: Lamuv.

————. 1982. *Das Vermächtnis: Kurzroman.* Bornheim-Merten: Lamuv.

————. 1982. *Vermintes Gelände: Essayistische Schriften 1977–1981.* Cologne: Kiepenheuer & Witsch.

————. 1983. *Die Verwundung und andere frühe Erzählungen.* Bornheim-Merten: Lamuv.

————. 1984. *Bild - Bonn - Boenisch.* Bornheim-Merten: Lamuv.

————. 1985. *Frauen vor Flußlandschaft: Roman in Dialogen und Selbstgesprächen.* Cologne: Kiepenheuer & Witsch.

————. 1987. *Rom auf den ersten Blick.* Bornheim-Merten: Lamuv.

B. English Translations

Böll, Heinrich. 1954. *And Never Said a Word.* Trans. Richard Graves. New York: Holt.

————. 1955. *Adam, Where Art Thou?* Trans. Mervyn Savill. New York: Criterion Books.

————. 1956. *The Train Was on Time.* Trans. Richard Graves. New York: Criterion Books.

————. 1957. *Tomorrow and Yesterday.* Trans. Mervyn Savill. New York: Criterion Books.

———. 1957. *The Unguarded House*. Trans. Mervyn Savill. London: Arco.

———. 1965. *Absent Without Leave and Other Stories*. Trans. Leila Vennewitz. New York: McGraw-Hill.

———. 1965. *The Clown*. Trans. Leila Vennewitz. New York: McGraw-Hill.

———. 1966. *18 [Eighteen] Stories*. Trans. Leila Vennewitz. New York: McGraw-Hill.

———. 1967. *Irish Journal*. Trans. Leila Vennewitz. New York: McGraw-Hill.

———. 1968. *End of a Mission*. Trans. Leila Vennewitz. New York: McGraw-Hill.

———. 1970. *Adam and The Train: Two novels*. Trans. Leila Vennewitz. New York: McGraw-Hill.

———. 1970. *Children Are Civilians, Too*. Trans. Leila Vennewitz. New York: McGraw-Hill.

———. 1973. *Billiards at Half-Past Nine*. Trans. Leila Vennewitz. New York: McGraw-Hill.

———. 1973. *Group Portrait With Lady*. Trans. Leila Vennewitz. New York: McGraw-Hill.

———. 1975. *The Lost Honor of Katharina Blum, or, How Violence Develops and Where It Can Lead*. Trans. Leila Vennewitz. New York: McGraw-Hill.

———. 1976. *The Bread of Those Early Years*. Trans. Leila Vennewitz. New York: McGraw-Hill.

———. 1977. *Missing Persons and Other Essays*. Trans. Leila Vennewitz. New York: McGraw-Hill.

———. 1978. *And Never Said a Word*. Trans. Leila Vennewitz. New York: McGraw-Hill.

———. 1982. *The Safety Net*. Trans. Leila Vennewitz. New York: Knopf/Random House.

———. 1984. *What's to Become of the Boy? or, Something to Do With Books*. Trans. Leila Vennewitz. New York: Knopf.

———. 1985. *A Soldier's Legacy*. Trans. Leila Vennewitz. New York: Knopf.

———. 1986. *The Short Stories of Heinrich Böll*. Trans. Leila Vennewitz. New York: Knopf.

———. 1988. *Women in a River Landscape*. London: Secker & Warburg.

C. Bibliography

Plant, Richard. 1954. "War's Aftermath in a German Town." *New York Times Book Review*, 17 October.

———. 1955. "Eroded Landscape." *New York Times Book Review*, 13 November.

Morton, Frederic. 1956. "Fiction Reviews." *New York Times Book Review*, 20 May.

Burger, Nash K. 1957. "Books of the Times." *New York Times*, 18 October.

Kopelew, Lev. 1957. "Ein Schriftsteller sucht und fragt." *Sowjet-Literatur* 3: 152–56.

Lauschus, Leo. 1958. "Heinrich Böll *Wanderer, kommst du nach Spa . . .*" *Der Deutschunterricht* 6: 75–86.

Phlippen, Anneliese. 1958. "Heinrich Böll: 'So ein Rummel.' " *Deutschunterricht* 6: 69–75.

Melius, Ferdinand, ed. 1959. *Der Schriftsteller Heinrich Böll: Ein biographisch-bibliographischer Abriß*. Cologne: Kiepenheuer & Witsch.

Reich-Ranicki, Marcel. 1959. "Bitteres aus liebendem Herzen den Deutschen gesagt. Der neue Roman 'Billard um halbzehn' eine große Leistung unserer jungen Literatur." *Die Welt*, 8 October.

Waidson, H. M. 1959. *The Modern German Novel*. Oxford: Oxford University Press.

Hermsdorf, Klaus. 1960. "Aufforderung zur Tat." *Neue Deutsche Literatur* 11: 144–47.

Ziolkowski, Theodore. 1960. "*Billard um halbzehn.*" *Books Abroad* 34: 238.

———. 1960. "Heinrich Böll. Conscience and Craft." *Books Abroad* 34: 213–22.

Becker, Rolf. 1961. "Böll, Brot und Boden." *Der Spiegel* 15 June.

Wagner, Frank. 1961. "Der kritische Realist Heinrich Böll. Die Entwicklung der 'Krieg-Frieden'-Problematik in seinen Romanen." *Weimarer Beiträge* 1: 99–125.

Jäckel, Günter. 1962. "Die Behandlung der Short Story bei Heinrich Böll. Versuch einer Interpretation von 'Wanderer, kommst du nach Spa . . . .' " *Wissenschftliche Zeitschrift der Universität Leipzig* 1: 609–12.

Kuczynski, Jürgen. 1962. "Zeitgeschichte in der Literatur. Arbeitslosigkeit und Not in zwei Werken von Anna Seghers und Heinrich Böll." *Neue Deutsche Literatur* 10: 110–119.

Lengning, Werner, ed. 1962. *Der Schriftsteller Heinrich Böll: Ein biographisch-bibliographischer Abriß.* Cologne: Kiepenheuer & Witsch.

Mandel, Siegfried. 1962. "Sabotage to Assert the Human Spirit." *New York Times Book Review,* 5 August.

P., E. S. 1962. "From the Bookshelf." *Christian Science Monitor,* 20 July.

Trahan, Elisabeth and Eva Schiefer. 1962. "The Imaginary of Heinrich Böll's 'Betrachtungen über den irischen Regen.' " *German Life & Letters* 15: 295–99.

Ziolkowski, Theodore. 1962. "Albert Camus and Heinrich Böll." *Modern Language Notes* 2: 282–91.

Reich-Ranicki, Marcel. 1963. "Der Poet der unbewältigten Vergangenheit." *Deutsche Literatur in West und Ost.* Munich: Piper. 120–42.

Haase, Horst. 1964. "Charakter und Funktion der zentralen Symbolik in Heinrich Bölls Roman 'Billard um halbzehn.' " *Weimarer Beiträge* 10: 219–26.

Hermsdorf, Klaus. 1964. "Problematisches Bekenntnis zum Nichts." *Neue Deutsche Literatur* 1: 136–39.

Reich-Ranicki, Marcel. 1964. "Mit verstellter Stimme." *Die Zeit,* 18 September.

Enright, D. J. 1965. "Artist Into Beggar." *New York Review of Books,* 31 January.

Koch, Stephen. 1965. "Outgrowing Germany." *Nation,* 3 May.

Lask, Thomas. 1965. "Books of the Times." *New York Times,* 25 January.

Vonnegut, Kurt, Jr. 1965. "The Unsaid Says Much." *New York Times Book Review,* 12 September.

Wensberg, Eric. 1965. "Books of the Times." *New York Times,* 6 September.

Bauke, J. P. 1966. "Watcher On the Rhine." *New York Times Book Review,* 16 October.

Beckel, Albrecht. 1966. *Mensch, Gesellschaft, Kirche bei Heinrich Böll. Mit einem Beitrag von Heinrich Böll: Interview mit mir selbst.* Fromm: Osnabrück.

Daniels, Karlheinz. 1966. "Zur Problematik des Dichterischen bei Heinrich Böll." *Moderna Språk (Language Monographs):* 25–32.

Fetzer, John. 1967. "The Scales of Injustice: Comments on Heinrich Böll's 'Die Waage der Baleks.' " *German Quarterly* 42: 472–79.

Korlén, Gustav. 1967. "Heinrich Böll in schwedischer Sicht." *Moderna Språk* 6: 374–79.

Reid, James H. 1967. "Time in the Works of Heinrich Böll." *Modern Language Review* 62: 476–86.

Sokel, Walter. 1967. "Perspective and Dualism in the Novels of Heinrich Böll." *The Contemporary Novel in German.* Ed. Robert H. Heitner. Austin & London: University of Texas Press. 9–35.

Wirth, Günter. 1967. *Heinrich Böll. Essayistische Studie über religiöse und gesellschaftliche Motive im Prosawerk des Dichters.* Berlin: Union.

Jäckel, Günter. 1968. "Die alte und die neue Welt. Das Verhältnis von Mensch und Technik in Bölls Roman 'Billard um halbzehn.' " *Weimarer Beiträge* 14: 1285–1302.

Jeziorkowski, Klaus. 1968. *Rhythmus und Figur. Zur Technik der epischen Konstruktion in Heinrich Bölls Der Wegwerfer und Billard um halbzehn.* Bad Homburg: Gehlen.

Reich-Ranicki, Marcel. 1968. *In Sachen Böll. Ansichten und Einsichten.* Cologne: Kiepenheuer & Witsch.

Schwarz, Wilhelm Johannes. 1968. *Der Erzähler Heinrich Böll. Seine Werke und Gestalten.* 2nd ed. Bern: Francke.

———. 1968. *Heinrich Böll. Teller of Tales.* Trans. Alexander and Elizabeth Henderson. New York: Ungar.

Thomas, R. Hinton, and Wilfred van der Will. 1968. *The German Novel and the Affluent Society.* Manchester, Toronto: University of Manchester, University of Toronto.

Daemmrich, Horst S. 1969. "Die internationale Situation der Germanistik. Die Germanistik in den Vereinigten Staaten: Studium und Forschung." *Colloquia Germanica* 3: 316–32.

Kuczynski, Jürgen. 1969. *Gestalten und Werke. Soziologische Studien zur deutschen Literatur.* Berlin: Aufbau.

Engels, Friedrich. 1969–1975. "Brief an Margaret Harkness." *Karl Marx, Friedrich Engels: Werke.* Berlin: Dietz (Institut für Marxismus-Leninismus beim ZK der SED). 37: 44.

Marx, Karl. 1969–1975. "Über P.-J. Proudhon (Brief an J. B. von Schweitzer 1865)." *Karl Marx, Friedrich Engels: Werke.* Berlin: Dietz (Institut für Marxismus-Leninismus beim ZK der SED). 16: 371.

Bernhard, Hans Joachim. 1970. *Die Romane Heinrich Bölls. Gesellschaftskritik und Gemeinschaftsutopie.* Berlin: Rütten & Loening.

Demetz, Peter. 1970. *Die süße Anarchie. Deutsche Literatur seit 1945.* Berlin: Propyläen.

Kügler, Hans. 1970. *Weg und Weglosigkeit.* Heidenheim: Heidenheimer Verlagsanstalt.

Migner, Karl. 1970. "Heinrich Böll." *Deutsche Literatur seit 1945.* Ed. Dietrich Weber. 2nd rev. ed. Stuttgart: Kröner. 290–310.

Adorno, Theodor. 1971. "Keine Würdigung." *In Sachen Böll. Ansichten und Einsichten.* Ed. Marcel Reich-Ranicki. Munich: Deutscher Taschenbuch Verlag. 8–9.

Amery, Carl. 1971. "Eine christliche Position." *In Sachen Böll. Ansichten und Einsichten.* Ed. Marcel Reich-Ranicki. Munich: Deutscher Taschenbuch Verlag. 92–99.

Augstein, Rudolf. 1971. "Der Katholik." *In Sachen Böll. Ansichten und Einsichten.* Ed. Marcel Reich-Ranicki. Munich: Deutscher Taschenbuch Verlag. 75–81.

Bauschinger, Sigrid. 1971. "Wie stehen die Amerikaner zu Grass und Böll?" *Frankfurter Allgemeine Zeitung,* 1 December.

Best, Otto F. 1971. "Der weinende Held." *In Sachen Böll: Ansichten und Einsichten.* Ed. Marcel Reich-Ranicki. Munich: Deutscher Taschenbuch Verlag. 69–74.

Cases, Cesare. 1971. "*Die Waage der Baleks* dreimal gelesen." *In Sachen Böll. Ansichten und Einsichten.* Ed. Marcel Reich-Ranicki. Munich: Deutscher Taschenbuch Verlag. 172–78.

Durzak, Manfred. 1971. *Der deutsche Roman der Gegenwart.* Stuttgart: Kohlhammer.

Fischer, Ernst. 1971. "Engagement und Gewissen." *In Sachen Böll. Ansichten und Einsichten.* Ed. Marcel Reich-Ranicki. Munich: Deutscher Taschenbuch Verlag. 153–62.

Gaus, Günter. 1971. "Die politische Vergeßlichkeit." *In Sachen Böll. Ansichten und Einsichten.* Ed. Marcel Reich-Ranicki. Munich: Deutscher Taschenbuch Verlag. 114–18.

Goldstücker, Eduard. 1971. "Botschafter Böll." *In Sachen Böll. Ansichten und Einsichten.* Ed. Marcel Reich-Ranicki. Munich: Deutscher Taschenbuch Verlag. 247–49.

Grothmann, Wilhelm. 1971. "Die Rolle der Religion im Menschenbild Bölls." *German Quarterly* 44: 191–207.

Harpprecht, Klaus. 1971. "Seine katholische Landschaft." *In Sachen Böll. Ansichten und Einsichten.* Ed. Marcel Reich-Ranicki. Munich: Deutscher Taschenbuch Verlag. 82–91.

Hartlaub, Geno. 1971. "Metaphysisch religiös." *Frankfurter Hefte* 26: 792–94.

Heym, Stefan. 1971. "Das Establishment und die Verantwortung." *In Sachen Böll. Ansichten und Einsichten.* Ed. Marcel Reich-Ranicki. Munich: Deutscher Taschenbuch Verlag. 150–52.

Hohoff, Curt. 1971. "Die roten Fliesen im 'Tal der donnernden Hufe'." *In Sachen Böll. Ansichten und Einsichten.* Ed. Marcel Reich-Ranicki. Munich: Deutscher Taschenbuch Verlag. 192–97.

Holthusen, Hans Egon. 1971. "Wirklichkeit beim Wort genommen." *In Sachen Böll. Ansichten und Einsichten.* Ed. Marcel Reich-Ranicki. Munich: Deutscher Taschenbuch Verlag. 33–39.

Jens, Walter. 1971. "Lob der Phantasie." *In Sachen Böll. Ansichten und Einsichten.* Ed. Marcel Reich-Ranicki. Munich: Deutscher Taschenbuch Verlag. 20–23.

Kaiser, Joachim. 1971. "Seine Sensibilität." *In Sachen Böll. Ansichten und Einsichten.* Ed. Marcel Reich-Ranicki. Munich: Deutscher Taschenbuch Verlag. 40–51.

Korlén, Gustav. 1971. "Böll in Schweden." *In Sachen Böll. Ansichten und Einsichten.* Ed. Marcel Reich-Ranicki. Munich: Deutscher Taschenbuch Verlag. 243–46.

Kurz, Paul Konrad. 1971. "Heinrich Bölls konservative Provokation." *Frankfurter Hefte*: 789–91.

Lenz, Siegfried. 1971. "Sein Personal." *In Sachen Böll. Ansichten und Einsichten.* Ed. Marcel Reich-Ranicki. Munich: Deutscher Taschenbuch Verlag. 24–32.

Lukács, Georg. 1971. "Lob des neunzehnten Jahrhunderts." *In Sachen Böll. Ansichten und Einsichten.* Ed. Marcel Reich-Ranicki. Munich: Deutscher Taschenbuch Verlag. 250–55.

Marcuse, Ludwig. 1971. "Neben den Erzählungen." *In Sachen Böll. Ansichten und Einsichten.* Ed. Marcel Reich-Ranicki. Munich: Deutscher Taschenbuch Verlag. 119–27.

Petersen, Jürgen. 1971. "Heinrich Böll. *Gruppenbild mit Dame.*" *Neue Deutsche Hefte* 131: 138–43.

Raddatz, Fritz J. 1971. "Elf Thesen über den politischen Publizisten." *In Sachen Böll. Ansichten und Einsichten.* Ed. Marcel Reich-Ranicki. Munich: Deutscher Taschenbuch Verlag. 109–13.

Reich-Ranicki, Marcel. 1971. "Nachdenken über Leni: Heinrich Bölls neuer Roman Gruppenbild mit Dame." *Die Zeit*, 6 August.

Sokel, Walter H. 1971. "Perspektive und Dualismus." *In Sachen Böll. Ansichten und Einsichten.* Ed. Marcel Reich-Ranicki. Munich: Deutscher Taschenbuch Verlag. 256–64.

Sternberger, Dolf. 1971. "Der Künstler und der Staat." *In Sachen Böll. Ansichten und Einsichten.* Ed. Marcel Reich-Ranicki. Munich: Deutscher Taschenbuch Verlag. 103–8.

Trommler, Frank. 1971. "Der zögernde Nachwuchs." *Tendenzen der deutschen Literatur seit 1945.* Ed. Thomas Koebner. Stuttgart: Kröner. 106–20.

Zimmer, Dieter E. 1971. "'Doktor Murkes gesammeltes Schweigen'." *In Sachen Böll. Ansichten und Einsichten.* Ed. Marcel Reich-Ranicki. Munich: Deutscher Taschenbuch Verlag. 205–8.

Ziolkowski, Theodore. 1971. "Vom Verrückten zum Clown." *In Sachen Böll. Ansichten und Einsichten.* Ed. Marcel Reich-Ranicki. Munich: Deutscher Taschenbuch Verlag. 265–75.

Zuckmayer, Carl. 1971. "Gerechtigkeit durch Liebe." *In Sachen Böll. Ansichten und Einsichten.* Ed. Marcel Reich-Ranicki. Munich: Deutscher Taschenbuch Verlag. 52–55.

Arnold, Heinz Ludwig, ed. 1972. *Heinrich Böll.* 2nd ed. Munich: text + kritik.

Bernhard, Hans Joachim. 1972. "Der Clown als Verfasser. Heinrich Böll: 'Gruppenbild mit Dame.' " *Geschichte der deutschen Literatur aus Methoden. Westdeutsche Literatur von 1945–1971.* Frankfurt: Fischer Athenäum. 272–81.

———. 1972. "Geschichte aus der 'Provinz'." *Der Schriftsteller Heinrich Böll. Ein biographisch-bibliographischer Abriß.* Ed. Werner Lengning. 3 ed. Munich: Deutscher Taschenbuch Verlag. 90–98.

Blöcker, Günter. 1972. "Der letzte Mensch." *Der Schriftsteller Heinrich Böll: Ein biographisch-bibliographischer Abriß.* Ed. Werner Lengning. 3rd ed. Munich: Deutscher Taschenbuch Verlag. 72–75.

Durzak, Manfred. 1972. "Heinrich Bölls epische Summe? Zur Analyse und Wirkung seines Romans 'Gruppenbild mit Dame.' " *Basis* 3: 174–97.

Grützbach, Frank, ed. 1972. *Freies Geleit für Ulrike Meinhof: Ein Artikel und seine Folgen.* Cologne: Kiepenheuer & Witsch.

Hengst, Heinz. 1972. "Die Frage nach der 'Diagonale zwischen Gesetz und Barmherzigkeit.' Zur Rolle des Katholizismus im Erzählwerk Bölls." *Heinrich Böll.* Ed. Heinz Ludwig Arnold. 2nd ed. Munich: text + kritik. 23–33.

Horst, Karl August. 1972. "Überwindung der Zeit." *Der Schriftsteller Heinrich Böll: Ein biographisch-bibliographischer Abriß.* Ed. Werner Lengning. 3 ed. Munich: Deutscher Taschenbuch Verlag. 67–71.

Korn, Karl. 1972. "Heinrich Bölls Beschreibung einer Epoche." *Der Schriftsteller Heinrich Böll. Ein biographisch-bibliographischer Abriß.* Ed. Werner Lengning. Munich: Deutscher Taschenbuch Verlag. 111–16.

Lengning, Werner, ed. 1972. *Der Schriftsteller Heinrich Böll: Ein biographisch-bibliographischer Abriß.* 3rd ed. Cologne: Kiepenheuer & Witsch.

Plard, Henri. 1972. "Mut und Bescheidenheit." *Der Schriftsteller Heinrich Böll: Ein biographisch-bibliographischer Abriß.* Ed. Werner Lengning. 3 ed. Munich: Deutscher Taschenbuch Verlag. 41–64.

Poser, Therese. 1972. *"Billard um halbzehn." Möglichkeiten des deutschen Romans.: Analysen und Interpretationsgrundlagen zu Romanen von Thomas Mann, Alfred Döblin, Hermann Broch, Gerd Gaiser, Max Frisch, Alfred Andersch und Heinrich Böll.* Ed. Rolf Geissler. Frankfurt: Diesterweg. 232–55.

Vogt, Jochen. 1972. "Vom armen H. B., der unter die Literaturpädagogen gefallen ist. Eine Stichprobe." *Heinrich Böll.* Ed. Heinz Ludwig Arnold. 1st ed. Munich: text + kritik. 32–40.

Waidson, H. M. 1972. "Die Romane und Erzählungen Heinrich Bölls." *Der Schriftsteller Heinrich Böll. Ein biographisch-bibliographischer Abriß.* Ed. Werner Lengning. Munich: Deutscher Taschenbuch Verlag. 31–40.

Wirth, Günter. 1972. "Tradition im Futteral. Bemerkungen über Böll und Stifter." *Sinn und Form* 24: 1018–1041.

Ziolkowski, Theodore. 1972. *Fictional Transfigurations of Jesus.* Princeton: Princeton University Press.

Conard, Robert C. 1973. "The Humanity of Heinrich Böll: Love and Religion." *Boston University Journal* 21: 35–43.

———. 1973. "Report on the Heinrich Böll Archive at the Boston University Library." *University of Dayton Review* 10: 11-14.

Friedrichsmeyer, Erhard. 1973. "Böll's Satire." *University of Dayton Review* 10: 5–10.

Glade, Henry. 1973. "Novel into Play: Heinrich Böll's Clown at the Mossoviet Theater in Moscow." *University of Dayton Review* 10: 15–24.

———. 1973. "Soviet Publications on Modern German Literature: A Survey." *Germano-Slavica*: 109–20.

Grothe, Wolfgang. 1973. "Biblische Bezüge im Werk Heinrich Bölls." *Studia neophilologica* 2: 306–22.

Ley, Ralph. 1973. "Compassion, Catholicism, and Communism: Reflections on Böll's *Gruppenbild mit Dame.*" *University of Dayton Review* 10: 25–40.

Murdoch, Brian. 1973. "Point of View in the Early Satires of Heinrich Böll." *Modern Languages*: 125–31.

Reich-Ranicki, Marcel. 1973. "Gegen die linken Eiferer. Bölls Stockholmer Rede." *Die Zeit*, 18 May.

Reid, James Henderson. 1973. *Heinrich Böll: Withdrawal and Re-Emergence.* London: Wolff.

Waidson, Herbert Morgan. 1973. "Heroine and Narrator in Heinrich Böll's *Gruppenbild mit Dame.*" *Forum for Modern Language Studies* 2: 123–31.

Ziolkowski, Theodore. 1973. "The Inner Veracity of Form. Heinrich Böll: Nobel Prize for Literature." *Books Abroad* 47: 17–24.

Arnold, Heinz Ludwig. 1974. "Heinrich Bölls Roman 'Gruppenbild mit Dame.' " *Heinrich Böll.* Ed. Heinz Ludwig Arnold. 2nd ed. Munich: text + kritik. 58–65.

Auerbach, Doris N. 1974. "The Reception of German Literature in the United States as Exemplified in the *New York Times* 1945 to 1970." Dissertation. New York University.

Batt, Kurt. 1974. "Die Exekution des Erzählers." *Revolte Intern.* Ed. Kurt Batt. Leipzig: Reclam. 191–274.

———. 1974. "Revolte intern. Betrachtungen zur Literatur der Bundesrepublik Deutschland." *Revolte Intern.* Ed. Kurt Batt. Leipzig: Reclam. 5–52.

———. 1974. "Zwischen Idylle und Metropole. Sozialtyp und Erzählform in westdeutschen Romanen." *Revolte Intern.* Ed. Kurt Batt. Leipzig: Reclam. 141–72.

Friedrichsmeyer, Erhard. 1974. *The Major Works of Heinrich Böll: A Critical Commentary.* New York: Monarch.

Habe, Hans. 1974. "Requiem auf Heinrich Böll. Zu seinem Buch 'Die verlorene Ehre der Katharina Blum'." *Welt am Sonntag*, 18 August.

Jeziorkowski, Klaus. 1974. "Heinrich Böll als politischer Autor." *University of Dayton Review* 11: 41–50.

Kaiser, Joachim. 1974. "Heinrich Böll. *Die verlorene Ehre der Katharina Blum.*" *Süddeutsche Zeitung*, 10 August.

Michaelis, Rolf. 1974. "Der gute Mensch von Gemmelsbroich. Heinrich Bölls Erzählung *Die verlorene Ehre der Katharina Blum.*" *Die Zeit*, 9 August.

Reich-Ranicki, Marcel. 1974. "Der deutschen Gegenwart mitten ins Herz. Eine unpathetische Anklage: Heinrich Bölls Erzählung 'Die verlorene Ehre der Katharina Blum.' " *Frankfurter Allgemeine Zeitung*, 24 August.

Schütte, Wolfram. 1974. "Notwehr, Widerstand und Selbstrettung. Heinrich Bölls Erzählung *Die verlorene Ehre der Katharina Blum*." *Frankfurter Rundschau*, 8 October.

Sölle, Dorothee. 1974. "Heinrich Böll und die Eskalation der Gewalt." *Merkur* 316: 885–87.

Stewart, Keith. 1974. "The American Reviews of Heinrich Böll." *University of Dayton Review* 2: 5–10.

Vogt, Jochen. 1974. "Das falsche Gewicht. Oder vom armen H.B., der unter die Literaturpädogogen gefallen ist." *Korrekturen. Versuche zum Literaturunterricht*. Munich: text + kritik. 99–108.

Anonymous. 1975. "*The Lost Honor of Katharina Blum*." *New Yorker*, 19 May.

Arbeitsgruppe. 1975. "Böll in Reutlingen. Eine demoskopische Untersuchung zur Verbreitung eines erfolgreichen Autors." *Literatur und Leser. Theorien und Modelle zur Rezeption literarischer Werke*. Ed. Gunter Grimm. Stuttgart: Reclam. 240–71.

Baker, Donna. 1975. "Nazism and the Petit Bourgeois Protagonist: The Novels of Grass, Böll, and Mann." *New German Critique* 5: 77–105.

Balzer, Bernd. 1975. "Einigkeit der Einzelgänger?" *Die Subversive Madonna. Ein Schlüssel zum Werk Heinrich Bölls*. Ed. Renate Matthaei. Cologne: Kiepenheuer & Witsch. 11–33.

Benn, Maurice. 1975. "Heinrich Bölls Kurzgeschichten." *Böll. Untersuchungen zum Werk*. Ed. Manfred Jurgensen. Munich & Bern: Francke. 165–79.

Bernáth, Arpád. 1975. "Zur Stellung des Romans *Gruppenbild mit Dame* in Bölls Werk." *Die Subversive Madonna. Ein Schlüssel zum Werk Heinrich Bölls*. Ed. Renate Matthaei. Cologne: Kiepenheuer & Witsch. 34–57.

Bernhard, Hans Joachim. 1975. "Es gibt sie nicht und es gibt sie. Zur Stellung der Hauptfigur in der epischen Konzeption des Romans 'Gruppenbild mit Dame.' " *Die Subversive Madonna. Ein Schlüssel zum Werk Heinrich Bölls*. Ed. Renate Matthaei. Cologne: Kiepenheuer & Witsch. 58–81.

———. 1975. "Zu poetischen Grundpositionen Heinrich Bölls." *Böll. Untersuchungen zum Werk*. Ed. Manfred Jurgensen. Queensland Studies in German Language and Literature. Munich, Berne: Francke. 77–92.

Beth, Hanno, ed. 1975. *Heinrich Böll. Eine Einführung in das Gesamtwerk in Einzelinterpretationen*. Kronberg/Taunus: Scriptor.

————. 1975. "Trauer zu dritt und mehreren." *Heinrich Böll. Eine Einführung in das Gesamtwerk in Einzelinterpretationen*. Ed. Hanno Beth. Kronberg: Scriptor. 139–49.

Cook, Bruce. 1975. "Brief But Not Slight." *New Republic*, 26 April.

Durzak, Manfred. 1975. "Entfaltung oder Reduktion des Erzählers? Vom 'Verf.' des 'Gruppenbildes' zum Berichterstatter der 'Katharina Blum.' " *Böll. Untersuchungen zum Werk*. Ed. Manfred Jurgensen. Munich & Bern: Francke. 31–53.

————. 1975. "Leistungsverweigerung oder Utopie?" *Die Subversive Madonna. Ein Schlüssel zum Werk Heinrich Bölls*. Ed. Renate Matthaei. Pocket. Cologne: Kiepenheuer & Witsch. 82–99.

Glaser, Hermann. 1975. "Bölls Aufsätze, Kritiken, Reden." *Heinrich Böll. Eine Einführung in das Gesamtwerk in Einzelinterpretationen*. Ed. Hanno Beth. Kronberg: Scriptor. 103–16.

Hinck, Walter. 1975. "Bölls *Ansichten eines Clowns* heute." *Böll. Untersuchungen zum Werk*. Ed. Manfred Jurgensen. Bern & Munich: Francke. 11–29.

Hübner, Raoul. 1975. "Der diffamiert-integrierte 'Anarchismus.' Zu Heinrich Bölls Erfolgsroman *Gruppenbild mit Dame*." *Ansätze zu einer Verbraucherpoetik*. Ed. Heinz Ludwig Arnold. Klett: Stuttgart. 113–44.

Jeziorkowski, Klaus. 1975. "Heinrich Böll. Die Syntax des Humanen." *Zeitkritische Romane des 20. Jahrhunderts. Gesellschaft in Kritik der deutschen Literatur*. Ed. Hans Wagener. Stuttgart: Reclam. 301–17.

Jurgensen, Manfred. 1975. *Böll. Untersuchungen zum Werk*. Vol. 5 of *Queensland Studies in German Language and Literature*. Bern & Munich: Francke.

Just, Georg. 1975. "Ästhetik des Humanen - oder Humanum der Ästhetik? Zur Heiligenlegende von der Leni G." *Böll. Untersuchungen zum Werk*. Ed. Manfred Jurgensen. Munich & Bern: Francke. 55–76.

Lange, Victor. 1975. "Erzählen als moralisches Geschäft." *Die Subversive Madonna. Ein Schlüssel zum Werk Heinrich Bölls*. Ed. Renate Matthaei. Cologne: Kiepenheuer & Witsch. 100–25.

Matthaei, Renate, ed. 1975. *Die subversive Madonna. Ein Schlüssel zum Werk Heinrich Bölls*. Pocket. Cologne: Kiepenheuer & Witsch.

Noble, C. A. M. 1975. "Die Ansichten eines Clowns und ihre Stellung in Bölls epischer Entwicklung." *Böll. Untersuchungen zum Werk*. Ed. Manfred Jurgensen. Munich & Bern: Francke. 153–64.

Reich-Ranicki, Marcel. 1975. "Vom armen Heinrich Böll." *Frankfurter Allgemeine Zeitung*, 20 September.

Rosenthal, Erwin Theodor. 1975. "Böll in Brasilien." *Böll. Untersuchungen zum Werk*. Ed. Manfred Jurgensen. Bern & Munich: Francke. 147–52.

Schelsky, Helmut. 1975. "Heinrich Böll-Kardinal und Märtyrer." *Die Arbeit tun die anderen. Klassenkampf und Priesterherrschaft der Intellektuellen*. Ed. Helmut Schelsky. Opladen: Westdeutscher Verlag. 342–63.

Schütt, Peter. 1975. "Ich habe eine Hoffnung, eine hartnäckige Hoffnung . . ." *Heinrich Böll. Eine Einführung in das Gesamtwerk in Einzelinterpretationen*. Ed. Hanno Beth. Kronberg/Taunus: Scriptor. 125–38.

Smith, Stephen. 1975. "Schizos Vernissage und die Treue der Liebe." *Heinrich Böll. Eine Einführung in das Gesamtwerk in Einzelinterpretationen*. Ed. Hanno Beth. Kronberg/Taunus: Scriptor. 103–5.

Wellershoff, Dieter. 1975. "Heinrich Böll *Gruppenbild mit Dame*. Ein Interview." *Die subversive Madonna. Ein Schlüssel zum Werk Heinrich Bölls*. Ed. Renate Matthaei. Cologne: Kiepenheuer & Witsch. 141–55.

Wirth, Günter. 1975. "Plädoyer für das Erbarmen." *Böll. Untersuchungen zum Werk*. Ed. Manfred Jurgensen. Munich & Bern: Francke. 93–109.

Wood, Michael. 1975. "*A Sorrow Beyond Dreams - The Lost Honor of Katharina Blum* - Separated by a generation, joined by Kafka." *New York Times Book Review*, 27 April.

Ziolkowski, Theodore. 1975. "Typologie und 'Einfache Form' in *Gruppenbild mit Dame*." *Die subversive Madonna. Ein Schlüssel zum Werk Heinrich Bölls*. Ed. Renate Matthaei. Cologne: Kiepenheuer & Witsch. 123–40.

Beck, Evelyn T. 1976. "A Feminist Critique of Böll's *Ansichten eines Clowns*." *University of Dayton Review* 12: 19–24.

Bohrer, Karl Heinz. 1976. "Moralismus und Kunst. Ein englischer Germanist übt scharfe Kritik an der deutschen Gegenwartskultur." *Frankfurter Allgemeine Zeitung*, 12 February.

Durzak, Manfred. 1976. "Die problematische Wiedereinsetzung des Erzählers. Heinrich Bölls Romane." *Gespräche über den Roman. Formbestimmungen und Analysen*. Ed. Manfred Durzak. Frankfurt: Suhrkamp. 154–76.

Ghurye, Charlotte W. 1976. *The Writer and Society. Studies in the Fiction of Günter Grass and Heinrich Böll*. Bern & Frankfurt: Lang.

Kafitz, Dieter. 1976. "Formtradition und religiöses Ethos. Zur Realismuskonzeption Heinrich Bölls." *Deutschunterricht* 6 : 69–85.

Kopelev, Lev. 1976. "Heinrich Böll und Wir." *Verwandt und verfremdet. Essays zur Literatur der Bundesrepublik und der DDR*. Ed. Lev Kopelev. Frankfurt: Fischer. 63–91.

Nägele, Rainer. 1976. "Aspects of the Reception of Heinrich Böll." *New German Critique*: 45–68.

———. 1976. *Heinrich Böll: Einführung in das Werk und in die Forschung.* Frankfurt: Athenäum-Fischer.

Sander, Volkmar. 1976. "Zur Rezeption der deutschen Literatur in der New York Times." *Die USA und Deutschland. Wechseitige Spiegelungen in der Literatur der Gegenwart.* Ed. Wolfgang Paulsen. Bern & Munich: Francke. 160–73.

Stern, Joseph Peter. 1976. "An Honourable Man." *Times Literary Supplement*, 30 January.

Ziolkowski, Theodore. 1976. "The Author as Advocatus Dei in Heinrich Böll's *Group Portrait with Lady.*" *University of Dayton Review* 12: 7–18.

Balzer, Bernd. 1977. "Anarchie und Zärtlichkeit." *Heinrich Böll: Werke. Romane und Erzählungen 1. 1947–1951.* Cologne: Middelhauve/Kiepenheuer & Witsch. 9–126.

Broyard, Anatole. 1977. "Missing Persons." *New York Times Book Review* 6 Nov. 1977.

Jenny, Urs. 1977. "Böll wählt die Freiheit." *Der Schriftsteller Heinrich Böll. Ein biographisch-bibliographischer Abriß.* Ed. Werner Lengning. 5th ed. Munich: Deutscher Taschenbuch Verlag. 91–98.

Kretschmer, Michael. 1977. "Literarische Praxis der Mémoire collective in Heinrich Bölls Roman *Billard um halb zehn.*" *Erzählforschung 2. Theorien, Modelle und Methoden der Narrativik.* Ed. W. Haubrich. Göttingen: Vandenhoeck & Ruprecht. 191–215.

Lengning, Werner. 1977. *Der Schriftsteller Heinrich Böll. Ein biographisch-bibliographischer Abriß.* 5th rev. ed. Munich: Deutscher Taschenbuch Verlag.

Masterton, G. A. 1977. "Heinrich Böll, *Missing Persons.*" *Library Journal*, 15 October.

Nägele, Rainer. 1977. "Heinrich Böll. Die große Ordnung und die kleine Anarchie." *Gegenwartsliteratur und Drittes Reich. Deutsche Autoren in der Auseinandersetzung mit der Vergangenheit.* Ed. Hans Wagener. Stuttgart: Reclam. 183–204.

Reich-Ranicki, Marcel. 1977. "Lebensgefährlich." *Frankfurter Allgemeine Zeitung*, 3 October.

———. 1977. "Mehr als ein Dichter. Heinrich Böll zum 60. Geburtstag." *Frankfurter Allgemeine Zeitung*, 17 December.

Zipes, Jack. 1977. "The Political Dimensions of *The Lost Honor of Katharina Blum.*" *New German Critique* 12: 75–84.

Wallraff, Günter. 1977/78. "Wir brauchen Heinrich Böll." *Literatur konkret* 1: 6–7.

Conard, Robert C. 1978. "Böll contra Brecht: 'The Balek Scales' Reassessed." *Perspectives and Personalities.* 101–9.

Kaiser, Herbert. 1978. "Die Botschaft der Sprachlosigkeit in Heinrich Bölls Roman *Gruppenbild mit Dame.*" *Wirkendes Wort* 4: 221–32.

Linder, Christian. 1978. *Böll.* Vol. 109 of *das neue buch.* Reinbek: Rowohlt.

Müller-Schwefe, Hans Rudolf. 1978. *Sprachgrenzen: Das sogenannte Obszöne, Blasphemische und Revolutionäre bei Günter Grass und Heinrich Böll.* Munich: Pfeiffer, Claudius.

Sammons, Jeffrey L. 1978. "Die amerikanische Germanistik. Historische Betrachtungen zur gegenwärtigen Situation." *Germanistik international. Vorträge und Diskussionen auf dem internationalen Symposium 'Germanistik im Ausland' vom 23. bis 25. Mai 1977 in Tübingen.* Ed. Richard Brinkmann. Tübingen: Niemeyer: 105–25.

Stötzel, Georg. 1978. "Heinrich Bölls sprachreflexive Diktion. Sprachwissenschaftliche Interpretation eines Interviews." *Linguistik und Didaktik* 33: 54–73.

Vogt, Jochen. 1978. "Vom Minimalprogramm der Humanität. Heinrich Bölls *Lesebuch.*" *Frankfurter Rundschau*, 14 October.

———. 1978, rev. ed. 1987. *Heinrich Böll.* Munich: Beck.

Warnach, Walter. 1978. "Heinrich Böll und die Deutschen." *Frankfurter Hefte* 8: 51–62.

Franklin, J. C. 1979. "Alienation and the Retention of the Self: The Heroines of 'Der gute Mensch von Sezuan,' 'Abschied von Gestern,' and 'Die verlorene Ehre der Katharina Blum.' " *Mosaic. Journal for the Comparative Study of Literature and Ideas* 12: 87–98.

Herlyn, Heinrich. 1979. *Heinrich Böll und Herbert Marcuse: Literatur als Utopie.* Lambertheim: Kübler.

Kuschel, Karl-Josef. 1979. *Jesus in der deutschsprachigen Gegenwartsliteratur.* Zurich, Cologne.

Moeller, Aleidine Johanne Kramer. 1979. "The Woman as Survivor. The Development of the Female Figure in Heinrich Böll's Fiction." Dissertation. University of Nebraska.

Reich-Ranicki, Marcel. 1979. *Entgegnung. Zur deutschen Literatur der siebziger Jahre.* Frankfurt: Deutsche Verlags-Anstalt.

————. 1979. "Nette Kapitalisten und nette Terroristen." *Frankfurter Allgemeine Zeitung*, 4 August.

Trommler, Frank. 1979. "Über die Lesbarkeit der deutschen Kultur." *Germanistik in den USA*. Ed. Frank Trommler. Cologne: 222–59.

Vogt, Jochen. 1979. "God bless you all and the Federal Republic of Germany. Heinrich Böll als Publizist." *Frankfurter Rundschau*, 14 July.

White, Ray Lewis. 1979. *Heinrich Böll in America 1954–1970*. Vol. 8 of *Germanistische Texte und Studien*. New York, Hildesheim: Olms.

Wirth, Günter. 1979. "Gefahr unter falschen Brüdern. Anmerkungen zum Charakter und zur Entwicklung der politischen Positionen Heinrich Bölls." *Weimarer Beiträge* 2: 56–78.

Bruhn, Peter and Henry Glade. 1980. *Heinrich Böll in der Sowjetunion 1952–1979. Einführung in die sowjetische Böll-Rezeption und Bibliographie der in der UdSSR in russischer Sprache erschienenen Schriften von und über Heinrich Böll*. Berlin: Erich Schmidt.

Göttert, Karlheinz. 1980. "Praktizierte Verständnislosigkeit. Eine kommunikationstheoretische Anmerkung zu Heinrich Bölls Terrorismus-Äußerungen." *Linguistik und Didaktik* 42: 168–176.

Holbeche, Yvonne. 1980. "The Rhenish Foxes: An Approach to Heirich Böll's 'Ende einer Dienstfahrt.' " *German Life & Letters* 1: 409–14.

Kesting, Hanjo. 1980. "Katharina Blum-Eine Romanfigur und ihre Kritiker." *die horen* 120: 86–97.

Krumbholz, Martin. 1980. *Ironie im Zeitgenössischen Ich-Roman. Grass-Walser-Böll*. Vol. 19 of *Münchener Universitäts-Schriften. Reihe der philosophischen Fakultät*. Munich: Fink.

Petersen, Anette. 1980. *Die Rezeption von Bölls 'Katharina Blum' in den Massenmedien der BRD*. Vol. 9 of *Text+Kontext. Sonderreihe*. Copenhagen & Munich: Fink.

Ziltener, Walter. 1980. *Die Literaturtheorie Heinrich Bölls*. Vol. 369 of *Europäische Hochschulschriften*. Frankfurt, Bern & Las Vegas: Lang.

Balzer, Bernd. 1981. *Ausfall in die Sorglosigkeit? Heinrich Bölls 'Fürsorgliche Belagerung.'* Frankfurt: Diesterweg.

Böll, Alfred. 1981. *Bilder einer deutschen Familie: Die Bölls*. Lübbe: Bergisch-Gladbach.

Conard, Robert C. 1981. *Heinrich Böll*. Boston: G. K. Hall.

Friedrichsmeyer, Erhard. 1981. *Die satirische Kurzprosa Heinrich Bölls*. Chapel Hill: University of North Carolina.

Hill, Linda. 1981. "The Avoidance of Dualism in Heinrich Böll's Novels." *Germanic Review* 56: 151–56.

Hüttel, Martin. 1981. "Böll in der Sowjetunion." *L' 80* (= Literatur '80) 18: 98–107.

Ribbat, Ernst. 1981. "Heinrich Böll 'Und sagte kein einziges Wort...' Ein Rettungsversuch mit Vorbehalten." *Deutschunterricht* 3: 51–61.

Sinka, Margit M. 1981. "Heinrich Böll's *Die verlorene Ehre der Katharina Blum* as Novelle. How a Genre Concept Develops and Where it Can Lead." *Colloquia Germanica* 2: 158–74.

Arnold, Heinz Ludwig, ed. 1982. *Heinrich Böll.* 3rd ed. Munich: text + kritik.

Bernáth, Arpád. 1982. "Das 'Ur-Böll-Werk.' " *Heinrich Böll*. Ed. Heinz Ludwig Arnold. Munich: text + kritik. 21–37.

Bogdal, Klaus-Michael. 1982. "Der Böll. Erkundungen über einen Gegenwartsautor in der Schule." *Heinrich Böll*. Ed. Heinz Ludwig Arnold. Munich: text + kritik. 126–37.

Eben, Michael C. 1982. "Heinrich Böll: the Aesthetic of Bread-the Communion of the Meal." *Orbis Litterarum* 37: 255–273.

Glade, Henry. 1982. "Gegen das Lukács'sche 'Rezept.' Anomalien der Rezeption von Heinrich Bölls Kurzgeschichten in der Sowjetunion." *Heinrich Böll*. Ed. Heinz Ludwig Arnold. 3rd ed. Munich: text + kritik. 138–42.

Herlyn, Heinrich. 1982. "Jenseits des Leistungsprinzips? Bölls Prosa der siebziger Jahre." *Heinrich Böll*. Ed. Heinz Ludwig Arnold. 3rd ed. Munich: text + kritik. 59–73.

Hill, Werner. 1982. "Persönlichkeitsschutz und Schmerzensgeld. Überlegungen zur Kontroverse Böll/Walden." *Rundfunk und Fernsehen* 1: 116–21.

Kügler, Hans. 1982. "Heinrich Böll: *Billard um halbzehn*. Zeit, Zeiterfahrung, Geschichtsbewußtsein. Zugleich ein Beitrag zum Lernziel 'historisches Verstehen von Literatur.' " *Deutsche Romane von Grimmelshausen bis Walser*. Ed. J. Lehmann. Königstein/Ts: Scriptor. 413–32.

Lange, Manfred. 1982. "Ästhetik des Humanen. Das literarische Programm Heinrich Bölls." *Heinrich Böll*. Ed. Heinz Ludwig Arnold. 3rd ed. Munich: text + kritik. 89–98.

Neuhaus, Volker. 1982. "'Strukturwandel der Öffentlichkeit' in Bölls Romanen der sechziger und siebziger Jahre." *Heinrich Böll*. Ed. Heinz Ludwig Arnold. 3rd ed. Munich: text + kritik. 38–57.

Reich-Ranicki, Marcel. 1982. "Spiegel einer Generation." *Frankfurter Allgemeine Zeitung*, 21 December.

Schröter, Klaus. 1982. *Heinrich Böll. In Selbstzeugnissen und Bilddokumenten*. Reinbek: Rowohlt.

———. 1982. "Zur Herkunft des Schriftstellers Heinrich Böll." *Heinrich Böll*. Ed. Heinz Ludwig Arnold. 3rd ed. Munich: text + kritik. 7–20.

Sewell, William S. 1982. "'Konduktion und Niveauunterschiede.' The Structure of Böll's *Katharina Blum*." *Monatshefte* 2 : 167–78.

Walden, Matthias. 1982. "Das Böll-Urteil und die Arbeit des Journalisten." *Criticón* 1: 80–81.

Ziltener, Walter. 1982. *Heinrich Böll und Günter Grass in den USA. Tendenzen der Rezeption*. Bern & Frankfurt: Lang.

Beyersdorf, H. E. 1983. "The Great Refusal in Heinrich Böll's 'Gruppenbild mit Dame.' " *Germanic Review* 1: 153–57.

Böll, Viktor. 1983. "Böll und Schlöndorff zur Verfilmung der 'Katharina Blum.' Gespräche." *Praxis Deutsch* 1: 64–67.

Class, Herbert. 1983. "Engagierte Zeitgenossenschaft der Literatur: Heinrich Böll in der Tradition politischer Publizistik." *Heinrich Böll als politischer Publizist. Drei Studien und ein Kurs-Modell für die Unterrichtspraxis*. Ed. Jürgen Förster. Bad Honnef: Keimer. 9–23.

Förster, Jürgen, ed. 1983. *Heinrich Böll als politischer Publizist. Drei Studien und ein Kurs-Modell für die Unterrichtspraxis*. Abhandlungen zur deutschen Sprache und Kultur. Bad Honnef: Keimer.

———. 1983. "Die publizistische Aneignung erlebter Geschichte." *Heinrich Böll als politischer Publizist. Drei Studien und ein Kurs-Modell für die Unterrichtspraxis*. Ed. Jürgen Förster. Abhandlungen zur deutschen Sprache und Kultur. Bad Honnef: Keimer. 99–123.

Friedrichsmeyer, Ehrhard. 1983. "Conard, Robert C., Heinrich Böll: Twayne (1981)." *German Quarterly* 3 : 530–31.

Jeziorkowski, Klaus. 1983. "Heinrich Böll. *Wo warst du, Adam?*" *Deutsche Romane des 20. Jahrhunderts. Neue Interpretationen*. Ed. Michael Lützeler. Königstein: Scriptor. 273–83.

Kirchhoff, Ursula. 1983. "'Die Suche nach einer bewohnbaren Sprache in einem bewohnbaren Land.' Korrespondenzen zwischen Heinrich Bölls publizistischem und dichterischem Werk." *Heinrich Böll als politischer Publizist. Drei Studien und ein Kurs-Modell für die Unterrichtspraxis*. Ed. Jürgen Förster. Abhandlungen zur deutschen Sprache und Kultur. Bad Honnef: Keimer. 24–98.

Kühn, Renate. 1983. "Zur Rezeption von Bölls politischer Publizistik." *Heinrich Böll als politischer Publizist. Drei Studien und ein Kurs-Modell für die Unterrichtspraxis.* Ed. Jürgen Förster. Bad Honnef: Keimer. 57–98.

Raddatz, Fritz J. 1983. *Die Nachgeborenen. Leseerfahrungen mit zeitgenössischer Literatur.* Frankfurt: Fischer.

Reid, James Henderson. 1983. "Back to the Billiards Table? Heinrich Böll's *Fürsorgliche Belagerung.*" *Forum for Modern Language Studies*: 126–41.

Beck, Evelyn T. 1984. "Ein Kommentar aus feministischer Sicht zu Bölls 'Ansichten eines Clowns.' " *Zu Heinrich Böll.* Ed. Anna Maria Dell'Agli. Stuttgart: Klett. 59–64.

Burgauner, Christoph. 1984. "Ansichten eines Unpolitischen?" *Zu Heinrich Böll.* Ed. Anna Maria Dell'Agli. Stuttgart: Klett. 117–29.

Conard, Robert C. 1984. "Heinrich Böll's 'Nicht nur zur Weihnachtszeit': A Satire for All Ages." *Germanic Review* 3: 97–103.

Dell'Agli, Anna Maria, ed. 1984. *Zu Heinrich Böll.* Stuttgart: Klett.

Durzak, Manfred. 1984. "Heinrich Bölls epische Summe?" *Zu Heinrich Böll.* Ed. Anna Maria Dell'Agli. Stuttgart: Klett. 65–85.

Fischer-Kesselmann, Heidemarie. 1984. "Heinrich Bölls Erzählung 'Die verlorene Ehre der Katharina Blum' und die gleichnamige Verfilmung von Volker Schlöndorff und Margarethe von Trotta." *Diskussion Deutsch* : 186–200.

Glade, Henry. 1984. "Friedrichsmeyer, Ehrhard. *Die satirische Kurzprosa Heinrich Bölls.*" *German Quarterly* 3: 503–4.

Janssen, Werner. 1984. *Der Rhythmus des Humanen bei Heinrich Böll.* '... die Suche nach einer bewohnbaren Sprache in einem bewohnbaren Land...'. Frankfurt, Bern & New York: Lang.

Kepplinger, Hans Mathias, Michael Hachenberg, and Hermann Frühauf. 1984. "Struktur und Funktion eines publizistischen Konfliktes." *Zu Heinrich Böll.* Ed. Anna Maria Dell'Agli. Stuttgart: Klett. 150–73.

Marianelli, Marianello. 1984. "*Fürsorgliche Belagerung.* Heinrich Bölls 'himmlische Bitterkeit.' " *Zu Heinrich Böll.* Ed. Anna Maria Dell'Agli. Stuttgart: Klett. 106–16.

Martini, Fritz. 1984. "Heinrich Böll - *Billard um halb zehn.*" *Zu Heinrich Böll.* Ed. Anna Maria Dell'Agli. Stuttgart: Klett. 49–58.

McGowan, Moray. 1984. "Pale Mother, Pale Daughter? Some Reflections on Böll's Leni Gruyten and Katharina Blum." *German Life & Letters* 3: 218–28.

Nicolai, Ralf R. 1984. "Zum historischen Gehalt in Bölls Erzählung 'Steh auf, steht doch auf.' " *Zu Heinrich Böll.* Ed. Anna Maria Dell'Agli. Stuttgart: Klett. 27–31.

Scheiffele, Eberhard. 1984. "Kritische Sprachanalyse in Heinrich Bölls 'Die verlorene Ehre der Katharina Blum.' " *Zu Heinrich Böll.* Ed. Anna Maria Dell'Agli. Stuttgart: Klett. 86–100.

Stern, J. P. 1984. "An honourable man." *Zu Heinrich Böll.* Ed. Anna Maria Dell'Agli. Stuttgart: Klett. 101–5.

Augstein, Rudolf. 1985. "Der unheilige Narr." *Der Spiegel,* 22 July.

Baumgart, Reinhard. 1985. "Götzendämmerung mit Nornen. Über Heinrich Bölls 'Frauen vor Flußlandschaft.' " *Der Spiegel,* 2 September.

Bernhard, Hans Joachim. 1985. "Bewahrung des Humanen." *Neue Deutsche Literatur* 12: 77–85.

Deschner, Margareta Neovius. 1985. "Heinrich Böll's Utopian Feminism." *University of Dayton Review* 2: 119–25.

Enzensberger, Hans Magnus. 1985. "Der arme Heinrich." *Der Spiegel,* 22 July.

Friedrichsmeyer, Erhard. 1985. "Heinrich Bölls Selbstverständnis als Satiriker." *Colloquia Germanica* 3: 202–10.

Götze, Karl-Heinz. 1985. *Heinrich Böll 'Ansichten eines* Clowns.' Vol. 18 of *UTB-Text und Geschichte.* Munich: Fink.

Jens, Walter. 1985. "Nachgerufenes, Erinnertes und Hinterlassenes-von der 'freundlichen Kraft' eines Wegbereiters und Zeitgenossen." *die horen* 139: 185–91.

Kaiser, Joachim. 1985. "Leiden und Größe Heinrich Bölls. Zum Tod des bedeutenden Schriftstellers." *Süddeutsche Zeitung,* 17 July.

Müssener, Helmut. 1985. "Erhard Friedrichsmeyer. Die satirische Kurzprosa Heinrich Bölls." *Monatshefte* 3 : 376–77.

Raddatz, Fritz J. 1985. "Seelen nur aufgemalt. Heinrich Bölls Bonn-Roman *Frauen vor Flußlandschaft." Die Zeit,* 11 October.

Rademacher, Gerd, ed. 1985. *Heinrich Böll als Lyriker. Eine Einführung in Aufsätzen, Rezensionen und Gedichtproben.* Frankfurt, Bern & New York: Lang.

Reich-Ranicki, Marcel. 1985. "Dichter, Narr, Prediger." *Frankfurter Allgemeine Zeitung,* 18 July.

————. 1985. "Ein letzter Abschied von Heinrich Böll. Aus Anlaß seines Buches *Frauen vor Flußlandschaft,* eines in Wahrheit nicht mehr abgeschlossenen 'Romans in Dialogen und Selbstgesprächen'." *Frankfurter Allgemeine Zeitung*, 8 October.

Zehm, Günter. 1985. "Heinrich Böll: Frauen vor Flußlandschaft." *Die Welt*, 24 August.

Baumgart, Reinhard. 1986. "Böll, Koeppen, Schmidt - Diese Drei." *Merkur: Deutsche Zeitschrift für europäisches Denken* 7: 555–64.

Bullivant, Keith. 1986. "Heinrich Böll - A Tribute." *German Life & Letters* 39: 245–251.

Friedrichsmeyer, Erhard. 1986. "Die utopischen Schelme Heinrich Bölls." *Amsterdamer Beiträge zur neueren Germanistik*: 159–172.

Höllerer, Walter. 1986. "Zum Tode von Heinrich Böll." *German Quarterly* 59: 103–105.

Linder, Christian. 1986. *Heinrich Böll: Leben und Schreiben 1917–1985*. 2nd ed. Cologne: Kiepenheuer & Witsch.

Rectanus, Mark W. 1986. "The Lost Honor of Katharina Blum: The Reception of a German Best-Seller in the USA." *German Quarterly* 59: 252–69.

Reich-Ranicki, Marcel. 1986. *Mehr als ein Dichter. Über Heinrich Böll*. Cologne: Kiepenheuer & Witsch.

Compton, Irene B. 1987. "Böll und seine Frauen. Ein Vergleich der Frauenfiguren im Früh- und Spätwerk von Heinrich Böll." MA-Thesis. University of Cincinnati.

Falkenstein, Henning. 1987. *Heinrich Böll*. Berlin: Colloquium.

Nielen, Manfred. 1987. *Frömmigkeit bei Heinrich Böll*. Annweiler: Plöger.

Ulsamer, Lothar. 1987. *Zeitgenössische deutsche Schriftsteller als Wegbereiter für Anarchismus und Gewalt*. Esslingen: Deutzer & Grosser.

Armster, Charlotte. 1988. "Katharina Blum: Violence and the Exploitation of Sexuality." *Women in German Yearbook: Feminist Studies and German Culture* 4 : 83–95.

Bracht, Edgar. 1988. "Das Bild des russischen Kriegsgefangenen und Fremdarbeiters in Heinrich Bölls Gruppenbild mit Dame." *Literatur in Wissenschaft und Unterricht* 21: 83–107.

Jeziorkowski, Klaus. 1988. "Die bewohnbare Sprache. Zur Poetik Heinrich Bölls." *Poetik*. Ed. Hans Dieter Schlosser and Horst Dieter Zimmermann. Frankfurt: Athenäum. 46–54.

Kaiser, Joachim. 1988. *Erlebte Literatur: Vom 'Doktor Faustus' zum 'Fettfleck.'* Munich & Zurich: Piper.

Perraudin, Michael. 1988. "Heinrich Böll. Approaches to Kleist." *Sprachkunst. Beiträge zur Literaturwissenschaft* 1: 117–34.

Rademann, Eckard. 1988. "Heinrich Bölls Amerikabild." MA-Thesis. University of Cincinnati.

Reid, James Henderson. 1988. *Heinrich Böll. A German for His Time.* Oxford: Wolff.

Schaller, Thomas. 1988. *Die Rezeption von Heinrich Böll und Günter Grass in den USA. Böll und Grass im Spiegel der Unterrichtspraxis an höheren amerikanischen Bildungsinstitutionen.* New York: Lang.

Sowinski, Bernhard. 1988. *Heinrich Böll: Kurzgeschichten.* Munich: Oldenbourg.

Streul, Irene Charlotte. 1988. *Westdeutsche Literatur in der DDR: Böll, Grass, Walser und andere in der offiziellen Rezeption 1949–1985.* Stuttgart: Metzler.

Wirth, Günter. 1988. "Engel von der Flußlandschaft." *Sinn und Form* 40: 437–51.

Cory, Mark E. 1988–89. "Some Observations on the Role of Violence in the Late Prose of Heinrich Böll." *University of Dayton Review* 19: 43–53.

Glade, Henry. 1989. "Die Rezeption der zeitgenössischen deutschen Literatur in der Phase der sowjetischen Perestroika: Am Beispiel von Heinrich Böll, Siegfried Lenz und Günter Grass." *Arcadia* : 303–13.

————. and Dorothea Mayer. 1989. *Sowjetische Verstöße gegen das Welturheberrecht. Westdeutsche Belletristik in russischer Übersetzung 1980–86.* Cologne: Bundesinstitut für Ostwissenschaftliche und Internationale Studien (Federal Institute for Eastern European and International Studies).

Jens, Walter and Hans Küng. 1989. *Anwälte der Humanität: Thomas Mann, Herrmann Hesse, Heinrich Böll.* Munich: Kindler.

Rademacher, Gerhard, ed. 1989. *Heinrich Böll: Auswahlbibliographie zur Primär- und Sekundärliteratur, mit einleitenden Textbeiträgen von und über Heinrich Böll.* Bonn: Bouvier.

Sammons, Jeffrey. 1989. "Germanistik im Niemandsland." *Germanistik in den USA. Neue Entwicklungen und Methoden.* Ed. Frank Trommler. Cologne: Westdeutscher Verlag. 104–20.

Vogt, Jochen. 1989. "Böll's Utopia: Great Refusal, Small Pleasures." *From the Greeks to the Greens: Images of the Simple Life.* Madison: Monatshefte/ University of Wisconsin. 111–26.

Balzer, Bernd. 1990. *Heinrich Böll, Die verlorene Ehre der Katharina Blum.* Frankfurt: Diesterweg.

Güstrau, S. 1990. *Literatur als Theologieersatz. Heinrich Böll.* Frankfurt, Bern & New York: Peter Lang.

Hynes, Joseph. 1990. "The Catcher on the Rhine: Heinrich Böll, 1917–1985." *Novel: A Forum on Fiction.* 3: 265–81.

Schirrmacher, Frank. 1990. "Abschied von der Literatur der Bundesrepublik." *Frankfurter Allgemeine Zeitung,* 2 October.

Stevenson, Diane. 1990. "The Temporal-Moral Matrix of Heinrich Böll's *Billiards at Half-Past Nine.*" *Twentieth Century Literature. A Scholarly and Critical Journal* 36: 95–114.

Bullivant, Keith. 1991. *New Approaches to Canonical Novelists: Heinrich Böll.* Unpublished Manuscript.

Jürgenbehring, Heinrich. 1991. "Liebe, Religion und Institution." Dissertation. University Münster.

Römhild, Dorothee. 1991. *Die Ehre der Frau ist unantastbar. Thetis - Literatur im Spiegel der Geschlechter.* Pfaffenweiler: Centaurus.

Vogt, Jochen. 1991. *'Erinnerung ist unsere Aufgabe.' Über Literatur, Moral und Politik 1945–1990.* Opladen: Westdeutscher Verlag.

Balzer, Bernd, ed. 1992. *Heinrich Böll 1917 – 1985 zum 75. Geburtstag.* Bern, Berlin, Frankfurt, New York, Paris & Vienna: Lang.

———. 1992. "Einleitung." *Heinrich Böll 1917–1985. Zum 75. Geburtstag.* Ed. Bernd Balzer. Bern, Berlin, Frankfurt, New York, Paris & Vienna: Peter Lang. 7–10.

———. 1992. "Das mißverstandene Engagement - der angebliche Realismus Bölls." *Heinrich Böll 1917–1985. Zum 75. Geburtstag.* Ed. Bernd Balzer. Bern, Berlin, Frankfurt, New York, Paris & Vienna: Peter Lang. 89–115.

Bernáth, Arpád. 1992. "Heinrich Böll als Hörspiel- und Dramenautor (Von den Anfängen bis 1961)." *Heinrich Böll 1917–1985. Zum 75. Geburtstag.* Ed. Bernd Balzer. Bern, Berlin, Frankfurt, New York, Paris & Vienna: Peter Lang. 61–86.

Bernhard, Hans-Joachim. 1992. "Böll als Leser." *Heinrich Böll 1917–1985. Zum 75. Geburtstag.* Ed. Bernd Balzer. Bern, Berlin, Frankfurt, New York, Paris & Vienna: Peter Lang. 267–85.

Busse, Karl Heiner. 1992. "Zu wahr, um schön zu sein - Frühe Publikationen." *Heinrich Böll 1917–1985. Zum 75. Geburtstag.* Ed. Bernd Balzer. Bern, Berlin, Frankfurt, New York, Paris & Vienna: Peter Lang. 25–41.

Cheng'en, Ni. 1992. "Böll aus der Ferne. Über Rezeption und Interpretation Bölls in China." *Heinrich Böll 1917–1985. Zum 75. Geburtstag.* Ed. Bernd

Balzer. Bern, Berlin, Frankfurt, New York, Paris & Vienna: Peter Lang. 305–14.

Finlay, Francis James. 1992. "Aspekte und Tendenzen der Böll-Forschung seit 1976." *Heinrich Böll 1917–1985. Zum 75. Geburtstag.* Ed. Bernd Balzer. Bern, Berlin, Frankfurt, New York, Paris & Vienna: Peter Lang. 315–38.

Friedrichsmeyer, Erhard. 1992. "Das weiche und das feste Herz. Sentimentalität und Satire bei Böll." *Heinrich Böll 1917–1985. Zum 75. Geburtstag.* Ed. Bernd Balzer. Bern, Berlin, Frankfurt, New York, Paris & Vienna: Peter Lang. 179–94.

Guntermann, Georg. 1992. "'Das Beharren des Verf. auf seiner alten Jacke.' Böll als Autor des verweigerten Einverständnisses." *Heinrich Böll 1917–1985. Zum 75. Geburtstag.* Ed. Bernd Balzer. Bern, Berlin, Frankfurt, New York, Paris & Vienna: Peter Lang. 195–230.

Herlyn, Heinrich. 1992. "Abfälligkeit - Kritik und Utopie." *Heinrich Böll 1917–1985. Zum 75. Geburtstag.* Ed. Bernd Balzer. Bern, Berlin, Frankfurt, New York, Paris & Vienna: Peter Lang. 117–134.

Hoffmann, Rainer. 1992. "Ausdruck humaner Wachsamkeit. Zu einem Heinrich-Böll Symposium in Köln." *Weltwoche,* 22 December.

Jeziorkowski, Klaus. 1992. "Die Schrift im Sand." *Heinrich Böll 1917–1985. Zum 75. Geburtstag.* Ed. Bernd Balzer. Bern, Berlin, Frankfurt, New York, Paris & Vienna: Peter Lang. 135–62.

Kuschel, Karl Josef. 1992. "Liebe – Ehe – Sakrament. Die theologische Provokation Heinrich Bölls." *Heinrich Böll 1917–1985. Zum 75. Geburtstag.* Ed. Bernd Balzer. Bern, Berlin, Frankfurt, New York, Paris & Vienna: Peter Lang. 163–78.

Vormweg, Heinrich. 1992. "Böll vor 1945." *Heinrich Böll 1917–1985. Zum 75. Geburtstag.* Ed. Bernd Balzer. Bern, Berlin, Frankfurt, New York, Paris & Vienna: Peter Lang. 13–23.

INDEX